Johrei seeks to build on Creation, rather than to distort or destroy it.

Johrei transcends sectarian or denominational boundaries; thus Mr. Okada's teaching fills a long-neglected void in the totality of human life. He wanted all people to know of this great power to induce physical healing and spiritual purity. And because his teaching never denies specific faiths, anyone can practice Johrei while remaining true to his own creed.

This book outlines a holistic philosophy of life and science, and a spiritual truth that can be applied in any area of the human experience.

The editors of this English version, Ichiro Nakamura and Teruyuki Tada, are both disciples of Mr. Okada. Mr. Nakamura is president and Mr. Tada is executive director of the Society of Johrei.

97-1174

JOHREI

divine light of salvation

Mokichi Okada (1882–1955)

JOHREI

divine light of salvation

Mokichi Okada

Society of Johrei

The Society of Johrei
131 Komatsubara Kitamachi, Kita-ku,
Kyoto, Japan
© 1984 by the Board of Directors of
The Society of Johrei
Printed in Japan
ISBN 4-915605-00-0

Contents

CONTENTS

From Night to Day
61

Johrei and Awakening
65

World of Perfect Harmony
71

Rewards of Penitence
75

Paradise on Earth
80

PART TWO: DYNAMICS OF SPIRITUAL HEALING

3 NEW FRONTIERS FOR MEDICINE

Spiritual Dimension of Health
87

Clouds and Toxins
92

Physical Effects of Purification
99

An Integrated Science of Medicine
105

4 THE WAY OF NATURE

Transmission of Johrei
113

The Nutrition Myth
120

Nature Farming
124

CONTENTS

PART THREE: PRAYERS AND HYMNS

CONTENTS

PART FOUR: LIFE AND THOUGHT OF
MOKICHI OKADA

APPENDICES

The character [*Hikari*] on the page following the frontispiece stands for divine light. Drawn by Mr. Okada,
it appears on the seal his followers wear. (See p. 120.)

Photos courtesy of Mr. Shigehisa Yamasaki (frontispiece), Rev.
Minoru Nakahashi (p. 116), and Prof. Hiroshi Hasegawa (p. 225).

Preface

THE Society of Johrei was organized in 1971 by the followers of the great religious leader, Mokichi Okada (1882–1955), who were closest to him. It is supported by member churches in Japan, Korea, and Brazil, and is dedicated solely to transmitting Mr. Okada's teaching throughout the world. Through the power lent to him by God, Mr. Okada saved hundreds of thousands of people from spiritual and physical suffering, in many cases from certain death, and led them to unshakable faith in our Lord the Creator. Although he passed away more than a quarter-century ago, his teachings continue to guide every aspect of our lives; and Johrei, the divine healing power that he brought to us, has been demonstrated to be effective in curing even the most serious of modern—as well as old —diseases. Members of our affiliated churches practice it daily to help the sick overcome their afflictions and to restore health in spirit and body.

Literally, Johrei means "purifying the spirit"; it is divine light transmitted to heal sickness or affliction, to strengthen and restore. Channeled through the palm of its administrator and accompanied by prayers, Johrei does not involve any therapeutic touch or laying on of hands. Unlike most other types of healing, spiritual or otherwise, Johrei can be administered by almost anyone, including lay believers.

This volume contains the essence of Mr. Okada's teaching on the theory and practice of Johrei. It is a description of the broad physical applications of Johrei as an art of healing, and it is also an introduction to a religious doctrine that gives Johrei meaning far beyond the level of simple faith healing. Above all, we hope this work illuminates the nature of Johrei as a divine gift and an intrinsic part of God's plan for the salvation of mankind.

The author's message is based on a series of revelations and inspirations that came to him during the last thirty years of his life, which were substantiated and elaborated through meditation, application, and experience. Mr. Okada wished all people to share his knowledge of Johrei and his understanding of God's will for man. That wish provided the original motivation for us to prepare this English version of his work, and it remained our main concern through the years required to complete it.

The present volume is a translation of selected passages from Mr. Okada's major works, including an unfinished manuscript entitled "Birth of the New Civilization." He was an unusually prolific writer as well as an untiring preacher; his writing and the transcripts of his sermons fill many volumes and cover almost every area of human life and endeavor. The passages translated here represent only a very small part of the totality of his work, but together they constitute a clear, comprehensive, and definitive statement on Johrei and Paradise on Earth.

To his followers, Mr. Okada personified divine love. His guidance has enabled them not only to overcome the sin of disbelief, but to learn of God's plan for salvation and to live blessed and joyous lives. It is our work as his disciples to make his teachings and the revelation he received available in English, eventually in other languages as well, so that many, many more people of all creeds, nationalities, and races will be able to share the manifold joys of repenting and returning to the path of God. Our purpose in publishing this volume is *not* to make converts to the particular tenets Mr. Okada expounded, and thereby expand our church organization; we wish only to make others aware of the power of Johrei and its provenance from faith in God. If one has that faith, Johrei becomes a universal vehicle for spiritual joy and physical strength that brings his life closer to the kingdom of God.

The task of translating the Japanese text into clear, coherent English proved to be unexpectedly difficult. It involved research, much discussion about meaning, writing and rewriting many times over. Early in the process we learned that literal translation does not necessarily convey the meaning of the original text accurately. In fact, word-for-word rendering often creates gross distortions and does no justice to the original text or to the author. Apart from the inherent differences between Japanese and Western patterns of thought, difficulties also arise from the heavy imprint of the particular historical and cultural milieu in which the text was prepared. For those reasons, it was especially important that we give priority to the intent of the author, the meaning he wished to convey, rather than to the letter of the original text.

Part 1 through part 3 are translations of Mr. Okada's original writing. The rest of the volume, including the introduction, was written by Ichiro Nakamura and Teruyuki Tada, the editors. Part 1 consists of two chapters where the author's religious ideas are presented. They are very important for an understanding of the spiritual premises of Johrei. Part 2, also two chapters, explains the theory of Johrei as an art of healing, suggesting how it might help to humanize medical science and direct it onto the path of genuine progress.

Mr. Okada was an outstanding *waka* poet and composed a total of more than four thousand of these 31-syllable verses. He chose several hundred of them for his followers to recite during services. Their content varies, but generally they express thanks to God, give praises for His creation, petition divine blessings, or respond to God's call for repentance. We have translated a selection of these verses for inclusion in part 3 to give some idea of the kind of prayers offered each day by the church members. Mr. Okada also stressed that if a prayer is sincere, and if there is a genuine wish for God's help, He welcomes prayers from anyone, anytime, in whatever words come most easily. In practicing Johrei one should pray as he expresses himself best, in his own language and in terms of his own religious experience.

Presented in part 4 are three articles prepared by the editors to describe the salient aspects of the life and thought of the author. A brief biography of Mr. Okada is followed by a bibliographical essay, which introduces his major writings. The third article, written by Ichiro Nakamura, is a short commentary on some of the key concepts in Mr. Okada's thought. We have chosen nine terms that are of special importance but are not fully explained in the main text, chiefly because the author assumed that no explanation was needed.

The two articles appearing as appendices A and B are research reports, one on Johrei and the other on nature farming, a method of cultivation designed to produce pure foodstuffs that Mr. Okada encouraged and directly promoted. Both are interim reports based on scientific studies conducted to date. It is hoped that they will be of special interest to scientists, particularly in the fields of medicine, dietetics, and agronomy.

In planning this volume, we were given encouragement and help by many individuals, within and outside our organization. Cardinal Arns, Archbishop of São Paulo, kindly granted us an audience in 1977 and enlightened us on the meaning of post-Vatican II ecumenicism and the importance of prayer in faith. Dr. Hajime Nakamura, professor emeritus of the University of Tokyo and Buddhist scholar of international renown, gave us invaluable advice on the most effective ways to communicate Eastern thinking to the Western intellectual community. The late Dr. Charles H. Dodd, joint director of the *New English Bible*, kindly imparted to us through correspondence his profound thoughts on biblical translation. Fr. Joseph Roggendorf, professor of comparative philosophy and culture at Sophia University in Tokyo until his recent death, was also a source of great inspiration and encouragement to the editors. We thank them all for their support in our endeavor.

While preparing the English manuscript for this volume, we consulted a number of theologians, specialists in the science of religion, members of the Catholic and Protestant clergy, as well as physicians, surgeons, and agricultural scientists. We are particularly indebted to Professor Richard Friedli, director of the Institute for Religious Studies, University of Fribourg, Switzerland, and his colleagues, including Dr. Anand Nayak and Fr. Paul Ihara, for their reading of the draft manuscript and their innumerable suggestions concerning basic theological issues. We have benefited greatly, furthermore, from the extensive knowledge of philosophy and theology that Dr. David F. Casey, a scholar of comparative culture, shared with us.

Among the many medical scientists who offered critical comments on the manuscript, we would like to express our special gratitude to Dr. Hiroshi Takita, chief, Department of Thoracic Surgery & Oncology, Roswell Park Memorial Institute, Buffalo, New York, and his colleague, Dr. Salvador Harguindey. Their candid opinions and penetrating observations were invaluable to us.

In the field of agricultural science, Dr. Hiroshi Hasegawa, professor emeritus of Kyoto University, has exercised skillful leadership for the past ten years in an extensive research project on nonfertilized fields. Without the cooperation of Professor Hasegawa and his colleagues at Kinki University in Higashi Osaka, it would have been impossible to complete the report on nature farming.

We owe our sincere thanks to many other individuals, including Dr. Hatsuo Nakamura, professor emeritus of Keio University, Mr. Yasuhiro Ōsaki, attorney-at-law, Mr. Shigehisa Yamasaki, specialist in art history, Mr. Frederick I. Scott, Jr., formerly editor of the *American Laboratory* and *International Laboratory*, Mr. Tsutomu Kano, editor of *The Japan Interpreter*, and Ms. Patricia Murray, executive editor of the same journal of social and political ideas published in Tokyo. Mr. Yoshiji Komiyama, senior managing director of the Komiyama Printing Company, and Ms. Susie Agoston, illustrator and book designer, were of great service throughout the production stages. The professional advice and technical assistance of all these individuals have made this volume what it is. Despite all the help we received from specialists in many fields, however, we, the editors, assume full responsibility for the content. Any or all errors of fact or interpretation, all stylistic or grammatical infidelities herein should be attributed to ourselves.

The publication of this work would not have been possible without the enduring support and encouragement of our church members. We would like to take the opportunity to express our most sincere appreciation of their help and steadfast cooperation. We are particularly grateful to Rev. Suzuko Nagashima of the Tokyo Reimei Church, Rev. Bok-soo Chung of the Mesia Kyohwe in Pusan, Rev. Minoru Nakahashi of the Templo Messiânico Universal, and Rev. Minoru Fujii of the Comunidade Messiânico Universal, both in São Paulo.

Finally, with sadness, we must mention the irreplaceable contribution made by the late Rev. Kenji Tatsumi, who, as secretary-general of our Society, devoted himself for years to this monumental project until his death in 1979 at the age of fifty. Rev. Tatsumi was a survivor of Hiroshima, and Johrei gave him the strength to carry on his mission for a remarkable thirty-five years after the atomic blast in 1945. In his deep faith in God, he was truly exemplary among the many disciples of Mr. Okada. A man of brilliant scholarly capability who was trained at the University of Tokyo, he abandoned a highly promising academic career midstream and turned all his time and energy to disseminating his mentor's teaching. His superb knowledge of English and his deep understanding of and keen insight into Mr. Okada's thought constituted an invaluable asset in our endeavor. Rev. Tatsumi was a man of faith who inspired us all.

Ichiro Nakamura
Teruyuki Tada

Introduction

MORE than one thousand people daily throng our two churches in São Paulo to receive Johrei. They come from rural and urban areas and from all walks of life. Among them are professionals and factory workers, people with Ph.Ds and those with only primary school education, men and women, young and old. Their social and ethnic backgrounds vary widely, but most interesting, almost all of them are Christians. Despite their commitment to faith in Jesus Christ, they do not seem to feel any internal conflict between their professed faith and their dedication to our church. Most of them attend mass regularly at their local Catholic churches, while they continue to practice Johrei and study the teachings of Mokichi Okada. Significantly, the congregation recites the Lord's Prayer at the daily services held in our churches in Brazil.

Many of the Brazilian members were suffering from incurable diseases or were under extreme emotional or psychological strain when they first came to our church for healing by Johrei. There, they witnessed extraordinary things happening before their own eyes; the instances of healing that took place among them were miracles. This direct experience with divine healing has been the most convincing proof that God is here with us, rather than "up there" someplace beyond our reach. The charisma of Johrei has enabled them to see and feel for themselves the working of God's mercy and power.

Our Christian members say that since they began to receive Johrei, somehow they feel God closer to them. Although they still see themselves as sinful and very imperfect, they are no longer held back by fear of Him as they once were. Well aware that He is not God of retribution but of love, they now have a genuine sense of awe that draws them ever nearer to Him. Some say that their new attitude has made them more devout as Christians than they have ever been.

Monotheism

The attitude of the members in South America in no way runs counter to the basic teachings of Mr. Okada. He believed that all great religions are manifestations of God's love and of His will to save man. He made it clear that although it may differ in doctrine, ritual, and organization, each religion in its own way performs the sacred task of guiding people to good and encouraging repentance.

For that reason Mr. Okada neither prohibited nor discouraged his followers from taking serious interest in or even embracing any one of the great religions.

He was so certain of the universal brotherhood of man, that a missionary effort to convert anyone who was already a committed believer of another faith did not seem important. As long as their belief is sincere, he taught, people can practice Johrei without abandoning their faith. His only hope was that their trust and faith in God would grow deeper through their experience with and knowledge of Johrei, the healing power of God channeled with prayer through the human hand.

Despite the broad latitude that characterizes Mr. Okada's teaching, our Roman Catholic members in Brazil would still have found it impossible to reconcile it with Christianity if the two religious doctrines had not shared something basic. There is little evidence indicating that Mr. Okada ever actually read the Bible or had any direct knowledge of what is written in it. We know that none of his secretaries or assistants was particularly knowledgeable about Christianity, or any other world religion, for that matter. Nevertheless, many of the concepts in his teaching are strikingly similar to those in the Judeo-Christian tradition. His ideas of God, creation, providence, man, sin, and the soul, to name a few, all have something in common with Christian concepts.

Mr. Okada taught that God, in His love, created the whole universe and everything in it, but that man brought terrible suffering upon himself by going against the divine will. God wants to forgive our sins, however, and yearns to save all of us. If we wish to be saved, we must repent and return to His path, seeking ultimately to become one with the divine. That means we must live in love for God, hence for our fellow humans.

In many other ways, Mr. Okada's teaching can be readily understood, even accepted, by Christians, or anyone. If Johrei is given by the grace of God, there is no reason to reject it. Further, Johrei leads both the administrator and recipient to directly perceive the presence of God and helps them enter into a deep union with Him. As a form of religious experience, it helps to broaden and enrich one's faith. It not only brings health to spirit and body, but also encourages a more thoughtful, caring life.

Secular Society

The initial response to Johrei by Japanese is usually less reverent than the sincerely respectful attitude of sanctity that most Brazilians quite naturally demonstrate towards it. The difference may stem from the polytheistic, syncretic religious environment of Japan. Neither of the principal religions, Shinto and Buddhism, incorporates the idea of a single, absolute, immanent and transcendent Being.* Through the centuries the two religions coexisted, accommodating and even blending with each other until the worship of nature, communal deities, and one's ancestors became the combined focus of religious life. Japanese are certainly not irreligious as individuals, but to most, the concept of one God, the Creator, is totally alien.

---

* This is not to deny that some of the Buddhist sects are henotheistic in their basic doctrine. It should also be noted that some Shinto theologians expounded monotheistic interpretations of the Shinto deities.

An important fact in Japanese history is that secularization had become a strong, deep-rooted trend by the end of the medieval period. Long before the mid-sixteenth century, when Saint Francis Xavier landed in Kagoshima to spread the Christian gospel, secular ideas already had strong influence on society. Records of the exchanges between Japanese inquisitors and Jesuit missionaries in the early seventeenth century, after the Tokugawa shogunate banned Christianity, also indicate how extremely rational and this-worldly the Japanese perspective was.

That tendency grew steadily more pronounced during the two and one-half centuries of national seclusion under the Tokugawa shoguns, and as the country began to modernize in the mid-nineteenth century, Japan became a predominantly secular society. Nonetheless, the traditional religions survived the Meiji Restoration of 1868, when the military government was replaced by a new regime under the emperor. With the appearance of many foreign missionaries, Christianity was revived. A new element, however, was the sudden emergence at that time of a great many so-called new religions. Most of them were either variations on traditional beliefs or outgrowths of folk religions. None avowed faith in God the Creator, and their doctrines were generally simple and relatively practical. Their basic tenets emphasized the many this-worldly benefits accruing to the believers.

New religions mushroomed again immediately after World War II to fill the spiritual needs of a defeated people, plagued at once by extreme poverty, hunger, and sickness. Like their Meiji predecessors, the postwar religions focused on this-worldly benefits. Most were destined to die out as soon as the war-devastated economy successfully weathered the reconstruction period to plunge into a long phase of rapid growth.

Internalization of Faith

Two questions arise from this brief sketch of Japan's religious milieu. First, what was the significance of Mr. Okada's teaching in the context of postwar Japanese society? Specifically, what did Johrei mean to the people who experienced its healing power as receiver and/or administrator? Second, how was it possible for Mr. Okada, a Japanese born and raised in a polytheistic tradition, to establish a doctrine that shares so much with the established monotheistic religions?

For our Christian members in Brazil, who accept God's existence as self-evident, there is no question that the effects of Johrei are all manifestations of His power. For most Japanese, on the other hand, God's being is not an *a priori* truth. Intellectually, they may know something about the Creator, but that does not mean that they are convinced of the reality of His presence. Consciously or unconsciously, they demand some tangible proof. The rather extraordinary things that happen as a result of channeling Johrei are usually more than convincing for those Japanese who come to us for help in their afflictions. They marvel at the healing power of Johrei as they receive it and begin to see clear signs of improvement in conditions that once seemed hopeless.

This initial shock, however, is only the beginning of a long journey for the Japanese who finally embraces genuine faith in God.

In most cases, the experience of Johrei and firsthand knowledge of the great power it embodies in healing gradually become incontrovertible proof of the existence of the transcendent being we call God. But most people do not immediately perceive God as anything more than an external object of worship from whom they can ask for blessings—the mundane benefits of prosperity and better health. Their own well-being and happiness are still their primary concerns.

Regrettably, many become so enchanted with Johrei as a method of healing that their awareness of God's presence does not develop beyond that point. But in many cases, sometimes aided by an intellectual understanding of the nature of God as love, a person who has the experience of Johrei healing is changed in his inner self. This is happening among increasing numbers of Japanese.

Another essential vehicle for the internalization of faith is practice, which includes meditation, charity, good works for the benefit of others, and prayer. Here again, the joyous experience of Johrei frequently leads a person to help others and tell them about God and His love for man. As Mr. Okada explains in chapter two of this volume (JOHREI AND AWAKENING), a person benefits at least as much by giving Johrei as by receiving it. In channeling divine light through the palm of his hand, the administrator. becomes the instrument of God. He must try to suppress all his personal concerns and sentiments, and be fully aware that it is not his own power, but God's, that heals. Apart from the physical healing, he and the recipient both receive spiritual healing. As his soul becomes purer and his faith becomes deeper, he can do better work for God. What makes Johrei truly universal is that not only saintly people but even the most ordinary among us can channel Johrei and heal the sick with wonderful results.

A much-debated issue in modern Japanese intellectual history is the identification of the conditions necessary for a universalistic idea to take root in Japan's soil and capture the hearts of millions. The question arises because not one of the imported systems of thought, including liberalism, Marxism, and Christianity, became truly indigenous, at least in the prewar period. It is thought that Christianity failed to penetrate Japanese society because its universalism clashed with the particularism of the traditional value system.

Placed in historical perspective, Mr. Okada's teaching on divine providence can be seen as an attempt to formulate and disseminate an endogenous set of universalistic ideas among the Japanese people. Using symbols familiar to his countrymen and demonstrating the healing power of Johrei, he tried to bring home the idea of God the Creator. What is most fascinating in this suggestion is that the attempt was made by a Japanese who had no noteworthy experience of another intellectual or religious tradition. Thus it is even more remarkable that apart from Christians and the small number of Jews and

Moslems, the followers of Mr. Okada's teaching are perhaps the only significant group of people in Japan who profess faith in God.

Historicity of Revelations

How, then, was it possible for Mr. Okada to construct a monotheistic doctrine without anything in the indigenous tradition to draw upon? The only explanation we can find is in the revelations and inspirations he received from God, directly and indirectly, beginning in 1926. Following Mr. Okada's teaching, it is our understanding that God has revealed Himself in various ways in human history and has intervened to shape the destiny of different peoples at different times. Why God chose Mr. Okada at that particular time, we will never know. He himself left no suggestion as to why, and so we can only surmise from the content of his teaching.

By 1926 Japanese society had reached a critical juncture where it could go to the right (militarism and fascism) or to the left (socialism and revolution), or take a middle way towards peace and democracy. It is possible that God intervened at that crucial point to tell the Japanese people through Mr. Okada that they must repent and return to His path if the catastrophe looming ahead for the nation was to be averted.

It is interesting that Mr. Okada predicted defeat for the Axis powers long before World War II had even begun. After the war he declared that the defeat was a positive good, calling it a form of purification for Japan as a nation. The catastrophe, he said, was the price demanded of the Japanese people for their failure to listen to God's call for repentance. It also offered hope— a new chance to work together to rebuild the country according to the principles of peace and democracy. In other words, God wanted to save Japan and its people, and Mr. Okada was chosen as His agent to spiritually guide the reconstruction.

Mr. Okada's mission went far beyond uplifting the spiritual state of a single nation. He had been divinely inspired to inform the whole world of the imminent divine judgment and God's intention to save mankind from self-annihilation. In order to survive the judgment, he taught, each of us must first reorient and reconstruct his inner self, and then reorient and restructure our civilization to remove from it the evils of war, sickness, and poverty. He envisioned a civilization that is perfectly balanced in its material and spiritual orientations, representing a wholly positive, constructive synthesis of Western and Eastern cultures. A country with its roots in Eastern culture, and practical knowledge of the West derived from a half-century of industrialization, Japan was perhaps well suited to play a role in the blending of cultures.

Mr. Okada said that his words were based on divine messages conveyed to him, but strictly speaking, not all of his teachings came directly out of revelations. The revelations he received, which are described in "A Brief Biography" (p. 161 ff.), radically affected his whole perception of man and the world. In consequence, it is almost impossible to clearly distinguish between Mr.

Okada's own message to his followers and God's message to man conveyed through Mr. Okada. The body of writing he left, however, indicates that everything he said on God, His nature and providence, the imminence of the judgment and Paradise on Earth, the healing power of Johrei, and the spiritual world is derived directly from revelations. Much of what he taught relating to human civilization, medical science, and nature farming may be the result of meditation and divine inspirations. Specific points in the diagnosis and treatment of particular diseases, and his discussions on morals, ethical behavior, social conduct, and human relations almost certainly came out of Mr. Okada's wisdom and experience.

One factor that makes his teachings difficult to analyze or categorize is his tendency to put forth a given idea in a number of different ways, depending on how much the particular audience could understand, the depth of their faith, and other circumstances. He could discuss the spiritual meaning of Johrei with a few of his disciples, but with people new to the faith, he tended to stop with an explanation of its physical working. The latter approach was useful in reaching people who might not have understood anything more abstract, but it created confusion among others. They began to wonder whether earthly paradise were not merely another utopia. Worse, the idea of spiritual peace became imbued with the suggestion of material rewards.

Mr. Okada wrote "Birth of the New Civilization" in his last years, with the intention of dispelling any misconceptions about doctrine among the believers, as well as providing for others a statement of what the religion stands for, its raison d'être, and our mission to spread the word of God.

Healing Ministry

During a quarter-century of an active healing ministry, Mr. Okada helped literally hundreds of thousands of people, saving many from death or vegetation. The methods he used had several strong similarities with those of a Christian ministry of healing, and some differences, also.

Mr. Okada emphasized the importance of words and prayer, as in Christian healing, but he ruled out physical touch as unnecessary. He was aware of therapeutic touch as a method of healing once practiced widely both in East and West, and he taught that when God created man, He gave a special healing capacity to hands. (The Japanese word for treatment, *teate*, literally means "touch by hand." The English word "treatment" and its German equivalent, *Behandlung*, also mean "to handle.") He never rejected the validity of the laying on of hands, but Johrei, the healing method Mr. Okada passed on, is different in certain aspects.

Johrei is a method of channeling divine light into the patient's body through the palm of the administrator, who holds his hand about a foot away from the area to which the spiritual power is directed (see the illustration). As in the case of the laying on of hands, it is crucial that the Johrei administrator know he is simply an instrument of God, and that he is *not* transmitting his

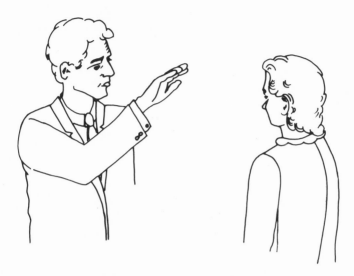

The Johrei administrator holds his palm about a foot away.

own power. Hence, his hand must be completely relaxed while his mind is concentrated on the well-being of the patient.

A group of believers led by a priest or minister often give prayers during Christian healing. In Johrei, prayers are said before and after the therapy by administrator and recipient, if the latter is a believer. Johrei is usually given in person-to-person sessions, but sometimes a number of believers assemble before the altar and give Johrei to each other. Mr. Okada also permitted qualified ministers to conduct group healing on certain occasions. At such times, the officiating priest extends his arm and passes his palm in an arc to reach out over the entire congregation. The motion is similar to the blessing by a Christian priest or Jewish rabbi, but a group session of Johrei is longer; it lasts for ten to fifteen minutes.

Another, more fundamental way in which Johrei differs from other methods of spiritual healing is that it can be practiced by anyone without much training, including lay believers. The laying on of hands, for example, tends to remain the sacramental preserve of priests and ministers. Johrei, too, is a kind of sacrament, but it is given as a gift of God to all people. Anyone can administer Johrei, and it works even when the practitioner has initial doubts about the efficacy of the method or even the presence of God.

Mr. Okada explains that Johrei is a symbol of God's love and forgiveness and of His wish to save mankind in this period of transition. It is a divine gift given man to help him prepare for the end of this civilization and the building of a new one. To be able to help in this unprecedented task, one must be pure in both spirit and body. Johrei is a power of cleansing as well as a vehicle of faith that can guide us to true health and wholeness. It is much broader in meaning and application than specific methods of healing physical ailments, emotional disorders, or spiritual abnormalities. It not only heals the whole person in body, mind, and spirit but helps awaken his soul to the absolute reality of God.

Purification

Mr. Okada's teaching on healing goes considerably beyond the bounds of religion. He introduces the concept of purification in order to approach health from a perspective that is as much physical as it is spiritual. Purification is a God-given function of eliminating alien impurities from the body as well as the spirit. The impure substances are explained in terms of spiritual "clouds" and their material counterparts, "toxins." Both clouds and toxins figure prominently in the theory behind Johrei.

In the course of a person's life, impurities inevitably gather in his body and accumulate here and there throughout. They tend to undermine his vitality and disrupt the normal functioning of his body system. Fortunately, the human body is endowed with the capacity to eliminate foreign impurities before they reach a point of saturation and endanger life itself. This natural function is what is meant by purification, and it is one of the many blessings God has given us. As impurities are eliminated from our body system, we grow that much healthier. The process of purification, however, is normally accompanied by symptoms usually associated with sickness—fever, pain, coughing, diarrhea, etc. Because of such discomforts, people have long failed to appreciate the crucial importance to good health of purification.

Mr. Okada advises against suppressing the process of purification. Certainly it entails certain uncomfortable symptoms, but we should let the process take its natural course and allow the impurities that have accumulated inside to be excreted. Johrei facilitates purification by eradicating the clouds and eliminating the toxins from our body, naturally and with minimum pain or irritation. Once the impurities are completely cleared away, purification is no longer necessary, and we will achieve true health.

On the other hand, if we suppress the purification process the accompanying symptoms will disappear, but only temporarily, and the consequences later are severe. It is technically easy to use artificial means to reduce fever, lighten pain, and stop coughing, diarrhea, etc., but that usually means blocking the elimination of impurities. Its self-cleansing action frustrated, the body will keep accumulating more clouds and more toxins. The long-term effects of suppression are beyond imagination; it can lead to serious afflictions months or years later, even in one's offspring. Mr. Okada warned that to continue to suppress purification will cause a critical rise in the incidence of complex syndromes that cannot easily be contained.

We believe that Mr. Okada's concept of purification offers some important clues to the enigma of the disease process. From the discovery of disease germs all the way down to research on the mechanism of cancerization, modern medical science has made tremendous progress in unraveling the mysteries of man's biological existence. There are, nevertheless, numerous basic questions that remain unanswered. Why is it, for example, that the same disease germs affect some people but seem to leave others untouched? Why do the same carcinogenic substances cause malignant tumors to develop in some but not others? How do we explain the wide range of conditions among the victims of a given epidemic, for example, or a food poisoning incident? These and hosts of other equally puzzling questions can perhaps be answered, at least better explained, by assuming that bacteria, viruses, or carcinogens are activated in the presence of toxins and clouds. For a further discussion on this point, we refer the reader to chapter three, where Mr. Okada elaborates on the concept of purification and other related ideas. Suffice it to say here that his hypotheses concerning the role of clouds and toxins shed light on the age-old questions of how to combat resistant bacteria, how to immunize oneself to infectious diseases, and above all, how to attain genuine health.

Alien Substances

Mr. Okada identified as a chief source of alien impurities in our body system any substances that are not originally intended for human ingestion. They include food additives, agricultural chemicals, medicines, and other matter God proscribed as non-food. Once ingested, they cannot be fully metabolized or excreted and take on toxic qualities over time. Hence, Mr. Okada was extremely concerned about the purity of what people ingest, and warned them against the use of drugs or medications—anything that contains chemical ingredients. He also taught that fertilizer is absorbed in plants and leaves a toxic residue harmful to the body system. The method he recommended to produce pure foodstuffs is "nature farming," which uses neither any kind of fertilizer nor agricultural chemicals.

Mr. Okada's warning against the abuse of medications pertains more to the future than the past. The history of medicine is very old, but only in this century have people been using medicines as much as they do today. Antibiotics, chemotherapeutic agents, and other superpotent drugs came into the picture just a few decades ago. Despite all the tests conducted to confirm their immediate safety, no one really knows how the doses of modern medicines taken over the years will affect one later, or the genes of future generations. Mr. Okada predicted that mankind would perish in due course if we kept on consuming substances that God did not create for human beings.

Today medical treatment and drugs are often the target of attack for producing dangerous side-effects or delayed reactions. Some of the charges are perhaps grounded in fact, but most tend to be exaggerated and ill-founded, rather than objective, constructive criticism. Mr. Okada had no intention of criticizing medicine at such a superficial level. He was highly respectful towards all the great accomplishments in the history of medical science. He believed that the fruits of science and technology in general have had a positive role to play in the unfolding of God's providence, propelling the advancement of man's knowledge and civilization. Mr. Okada's sole point of contention was the necessity to treat man as a spiritual-corporeal entity and appreciate the purificatory function of the body as a blessed asset, rather than a liability. He hoped that by incorporating the idea of purification into their understanding of the disease process, medical scientists would be able to open up a new horizon in their theoretical research and clinical studies.

Nature Farming

Mr. Okada advocated nature farming as a method of producing the foodstuffs that are necessary to sustain human life, maintain good health, and enable each person to perform his mission. He taught that God gave soil the role of producing foodstuffs and endowed it with the properties necessary to perform that task. Most important in farming, therefore, is to let the soil exercise its inherent properties fully, or conversely, to avoid anything that interferes with the natural nourishing power of the soil. By advocating nature farming, Mr. Okada was, in effect, urging that we reconsider the modern methods of cultivation that are heavily dependent on artificial, rather than natural, power.

It should be noted that nature farming differs from organic agriculture. Organic farming methods are gaining in popularity in many countries because of the spreading aversion to the use of chemicals in food production, but nature farming goes one step further by avoiding even compost and manure. This is not to imply that nature farming has been perfected, or is always workable. Practical and technical problems abound in applying this unique method of farming, depending on the region and type of crops. But it is possible that with the cooperation of agricultural scientists, most of these problems can be solved. Already a group of Japanese agronomists have been studying several fields in the Kyoto area that are being managed by the methods of nature farming. Their findings are summarized in "Research on Nature Farming" appended to this volume.

As disciples of Mr. Okada, we fervently hope that our mentor's ideas about farming will receive the wide recognition they deserve for their possible relevance to the agriculture of tomorrow. Nature farming not only has proven to be capable of producing pure foodstuffs that are ideal for human health, but it also conserves resources and does not pollute the environment. As mentioned in chapter four (NATURE FARMING), as well as in the appended report, this method has definite advantages. Rice plants grown in the unfertilized, unsprayed fields show great resistance to blast disease, for example, and the influx of planthoppers, both of which can ruin the entire crop of a manured or fertilized field. This last point should be of special interest to agronomists, biologists, and even medical scientists.

As with Johrei, nature farming is but one of the many ways in which Mr. Okada tried to demonstrate how our civilization might be brought back into nature's orbit. Although this volume focuses on religion, medicine, and agriculture, his teaching covered a broader range of human endeavor, including government, economics, education, and the arts. He consistently addressed himself to the fundamental issue of our time: how to save human civilization from self-destruction. The truth he postulated is often described as the middle way. By that he meant that the truth is both spiritual and material.

The middle way seeks to synthesize human civilization into a truly universal, perfectly balanced culture. Science and religion must be fully integrated to bring man closer to the quality and purpose of existence that God originally ordained.

From the point of view of a specialist, some of Mr. Okada's teaching may sound unsophisticated, and given the passage of time since the early 1950s, some of his observations may no longer be valid. We hope, nevertheless, that the reader will try to grasp the essence of his message, for it is too profound and too urgent to pass over. If the reader can free himself as much as possible from prejudice and established conceptions, he will begin to appreciate some wholly new ideas and truths that we believe this volume contains. And if any part of Mr. Okada's teaching should be taken up by theologians or scientists for further probing, part of our purpose in publishing this book will have been fulfilled.

Part One
THE ROAD TO SALVATION

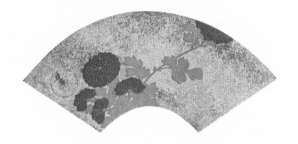

THE most important message in Part 1 is the revelation that Mr. Okada received concerning the imminence of Paradise on Earth. Again and again God has revealed Himself in human history and communicated His will to save man. The scriptures of the great world religions contain the revelation of God and His command that we return to the path He has laid for us. Still we have failed to respond to God's call for repentance, and by that failure we have allowed evil to penetrate deeper into our lives until it is almost out of control. The history of the world's civilizations has reached a critical juncture now, and the direction it takes will determine whether we, the human race, are doomed or will rise above our failure and achieve lasting peace and happiness. At this point God has once again shown His infinitely great love and power by inspiring Mr. Okada with the knowledge of Johrei. Here, the author describes Johrei as a divine gift, first and foremost, one offered to enable people to practice true charity and help them experience the presence of God. Potentially, Mr. Okada says, Johrei leads both administrator and recipient to become humble and repent of their sins. Those who do repent will be forgiven and permitted to join in the holy task of building earthly paradise, a new world of truth, goodness, and beauty where God's will is finally realized. Human civilization will then regain the perfect balance between spiritual and material, and man's soul will grow closer to God until it is ready for salvation and oneness with the divine.—Eds.

1

The Trials of Civilization

PROPHETIC RENEWAL

THIS is a small volume, but what is inside is of critical importance. The words within it reach out to all people and touch the future of all humankind, for they convey the will of God the Creator. These pages tell of a divine task carried on since time immemorial that is now nearing fulfillment. God has charged man with the magnificent mission of building a new civilization under His omniscient care.

I earnestly hope that the leaders in every field of endeavor in every society will read and take this work to heart, because their understanding of its message has great bearing on the happiness of all those who seek their guidance. I hope that people everywhere will read it, for it will awaken them and change them; it will lead them to a new perspective on the cultures man has fashioned and the roles played by religion and philosophy, science and art, and all else in human history.

Judgment at Hand

Civilization as we know it is only transitory; it will

33

finally pass away as the new age dawns and the true civilization is born. That will mark the end of the "provisional" world we live in today. God wills a reckoning for the old civilization and the establishment of a new one, and the time of His reckoning is at last drawing near.

Until now evil forces have had wide latitude in civilization, but in the transition from the old to the new, they will be weeded out. All people will go through an inexorable process of cleansing. The world will be terribly afflicted in payment for untold sins gathered over millennia. The great affliction is the sign that all societies and nations are being purified, and it will lift humankind to a new level of existence where good prevails.

The transition, which is actually upon us now, is the last stage before the beginning of an earthly paradise. In the upheaval, every sphere of life and every corner of civilization will be transformed.* Those who believe in God and repent will witness the coming of the new world, and they will be able to start on the road to salvation. But those still heavily burdened with sin and unable to overcome their malicious ways will end this life in absolute misery and may find no salvation in the next.

In His great love, God is warning us that we must repent, because He wishes to rescue as many as possible from the calamity that will cleanse the world. Through this testament I hope to spread God's truth every-

* See pp. 64–65 for a more detailed discussion of the spiritual upheaval. —Eds.

34

where, to confirm that a joyful future here, in the world, does indeed await all people who seek salvation and turn to God for help. Understanding the full meaning of the human fall from grace, those people will be able to start remolding themselves and their societies according to their deepening knowledge of the principles of the new civilization. Those who do not respond to God's call will suffer painfully, but by then it may be too late.

Signs of Hope

God now commands us to begin building Paradise on Earth. Perceptible signs of renewal are everywhere, but they are especially abundant in the extraordinary blessings that so many have received through Johrei. This, the power of the divine light, has restored the health and happiness of countless people who suffered from all manner of miseries. Before our very eyes, many of them have been saved from certain death or disaster. In these pages I will explain the working of God's providence in history, the significance of Johrei, and how God's plan is to be fulfilled.

With the advent of the new world, which will grow in magnificence, beauty, and grandeur, people will experience a life that brings only hope and happiness. They will rejoice in the assurance that ultimately God will grant them salvation. My message here is that God's plan is soon to be fulfilled in the realization of earthly paradise.

A Grand Paradox

Any careful study of the course of history cannot fail to confront the question of how evil* came into the world of man. First we must understand that God created man as good, but He also gave him freedom of will. He never withdrew that freedom, even when man chose betrayal and rebellion against Him. That sin marked the rise of moral evil and human suffering. All the generations have continued to disobey God, thereby strengthening the influence of evil forces in society. Nevertheless, God has consistently encouraged man to use all his resources to fight and overcome evil.

Legacy of Struggle

When we look back over the progress of our civilization, we find that it gradually advanced through a constant struggle between good and evil. The chronicles of the past are filled with wars and disasters. There are also countless instances of sincerity scorned and exploited by selfishness and guile, while cases of malice overcome by benevolence are few and far between. From primitive times, the powerful have harassed the weak, deprived them of their freedom, wantonly murdered, plundered, and tortured. This is not to say that power is inherently evil or that weakness is always good, but it is almost a

---

* The term "evil" is used with different levels of meaning in Mr. Okada's writing and speeches, but basically it refers to everything that contravenes God's will for man and His creation, either morally or physically.—Eds.

historical truism that the good are more often weak, taunted by powerful, wicked oppressors.

Evil's rampages have driven people to devise defenses of all descriptions. In an attempt to bring evil under control and guard against it, they have steadily built up elaborate legal systems and institutions. Democratic systems are one result of that effort. Democracy has never been perfected, but in many countries it has been effective in checking exploitation, the abuse of power, and social injustice.

Great religious leaders have appeared from time to time to guide people in their struggle against evil. They have left us a rich body of spiritually uplifting ideas and a legacy of humanitarian concern. Some propounded broad doctrines based on love, tolerance, and mercy, while others preached ascetic principles of resignation and renunciation of all mundane desires and exhorted their followers to obey, unquestioning. Many prophesied the coming of a better world, to offer hope for the future, but warned people that they must repent of their sins. Because of such leaders, the world religions have had enormous influence on man's spiritual life.

History has witnessed efforts by scientists, also, who sought through empirical and physical means to lighten human suffering. As a result of their labors, science has taken huge strides forward and civilization has reached glorious levels of achievement. Scientific discoveries and inventions have added immeasurably to the rich reservoir of man's knowledge and the quality of his life.

Spiritual Lag

Despite all those efforts, the influence of evil forces has not diminished. It has increased, in fact, to the point where human suffering is now monumental. It seems at times to be pushing our species to the brink of annihilation. That we have survived this far is only through God's grace; in His providence, He wishes to save us.

Expanding human knowledge has always held great potential for good. But it has also fueled the energy of those of evil motivation to invent cleverer and ever more cruel weapons that end up destroying peace and happiness. Evil use of scientific knowledge has made possible more sophisticated tools for maiming and killing. Atomic fission was a momentous discovery, but it provided the basis for making a bomb with a force so terrible as to threaten genocide.

If the human race is to survive, war must become an unthinkable thing of the past. Otherwise it will exterminate us. In spite of the ever-growing horror of war, nations still invest prodigious effort, talent, and resources in the attempt to increase their power to defend themselves or to defeat their adversaries. The arms race among nations seems to know no bounds.

In despair of the world's future, and with constant fear and apprehension in their lives, many thinking people are driven to skepticism, cynicism, or nihilism. Others seek solace in religion, or reach out for answers in philosophy, but more turn to science for solutions to their problems. Then, growing uncertain about whether science really can provide the answer, they come to a dead end.

In societies throughout the world, the balance between scientific progress and spiritual growth has been destroyed, especially in modern times, as people grow more and more skeptical about God's existence and the human consciousness becomes heavily preoccupied with the material. Science and technology have developed to maturity, while agnosticism and unbelief have overtaken the hearts and minds of many people. Atheism* has become an intellectual vehicle for evil, which, gradually superseding good, has caused endless tribulation and is pushing the faithless deeper into misery.

Triumph of Good

In order to remove the fundamental flaws of our civilization, we must ask specifically why evil, both individual and social, has been allowed to function in the world. If evil, especially moral evil, is the source of human unhappiness, why does God tolerate it? Why does He not punish all sin immediately?

It may appear to be sheer perversity, but it is out of love that God waits until each of us becomes fully aware of his own sinfulness and repents, to enable him to overcome the evil in his heart. We are saved by the grace of God's forgiveness. This is not a god of terrible retribution, but God of love, patiently waiting and wishing to

---

* Disbelief is a major sin subject to punishment after death. See p. 44. —Eds.

save instead of destroying. We are blessed, therefore, to have the chance for repentance and to feel the burden of our sins lightened when we are forgiven.

We cannot hope to prevent war unless we push away the evil desires in our hearts and ask for God's help to purify our souls. If we can do that and with God's grace begin to open ourselves to goodness, the very threat of war will have acted as a stimulus to change our lives, and the providence of God will have transformed a horrendous possibility into a force for good.

History shows that very often God's tolerance of evil has brought good by stimulating progress in civilization. Conflicts between good and evil in all areas of life have had their beneficial side, too, apart from the pain and misery they cause. In that sense alone, evil, the consequence of the human betrayal, has had an important role to play in the historical process. Its time, however, is limited by the will of God. The end of domination by evil will mark the final victory of good and the beginning of earthly paradise. Ours will become a world of truth, goodness, and beauty, where humankind is at last free from the three greatest of afflictions: disease, poverty, and war.

God wills that earthly paradise shall be the fruit of the labors of those who repent and whose sins are forgiven. By God's grace we must overcome unbelief and seek His forgiveness. Faith in God must be revitalized among all people in every community.

The time has come to check evil in all its forms, and let good predominate. This is not a fancy of my personal hopes or dreams; it is God's plan for the world, for all humankind. Our civilization will soon pass into the hand of good, for now we stand on the threshold of Paradise on Earth.*

THE REALM OF SPIRIT

Despite all its flaws, our civilization has come a long way, and there is good reason for its many achievements. This civilization should not be completely undone. Rather, it must be reformed and perfected by people who recognize the spiritual nature of creation and live and run their societies on that basis. The new civilization that will arise is premised on the realization of God's will; in it man will attain a harmonious balance between spiritual fulfillment and material blessings.

We, the human race, who are to transform our world and open its gates to a higher level of spirituality, can succeed only by accepting and drawing upon the power of the realm of spirit. Today, we too often pigeonhole material or physical phenomena into the slot of natural science, while we simply relegate spiritual experiences to parapsychology, or, when there seems to be no hope of rational explanation, to religion. The human mind can operate on both scientific and religious levels, but the two kinds of thought are often considered irrelevant to, or even incompatible with, each other. Still, the only way to grasp the truth about man and the universe is through

* For a description of Paradise on Earth, see pp. 80–84.—Eds.

an integrated approach that combines both scientific and religious thinking.

Dominion over Matter

To begin at the most basic level, all of creation owes its birth and growth to the power of God. He exercises His power through the realm that encompasses all the spiritual dimensions of creation, including human souls. We call this the realm of spirit—as opposed to the realm of matter, which comprises all physical, material aspects of creation. The two realms can be distinguished in this way, but they are not separate, existing side by side. The two are different dimensions of the same cosmic reality. The spiritual dimension transcends physical time and space, as we know them; thus the material dimension is contained by the realm of spirit.

One of the principles by which God presides over the universe and all His creation is that the spiritual always takes precedence over the material. The state of affairs in the realm of matter is ultimately a reflection of the conditions in the realm of spirit. The cause-effect relationship between the two realms is characterized by a temporal gap. Sometimes the lag is great, sometimes negligible, but on the whole, changes in the spiritual world are reflected much later in the material world. Any thought or deed, for example, is instantaneously registered in the realm of spirit, but its effects do not become apparent in the realm of matter until later, when they seem almost irrelevant to the spiritual cause.

The principle of spiritual dominance applies eminently to the human body. The soul is the center of each human existence; it determines one's spiritual state, which in turn affects his physical and mental condition. The sciences remain incomplete insofar as they fail to recognize the dynamic relationship between a person's spiritual and physical conditions. Science in the future must also incorporate many other laws that hitherto have been unknown or neglected. The principle of purification is one. According to this principle, as we will discuss later, contaminated areas belonging to the realm of spirit are cleansed, and this cleansing action is echoed in the realm of matter in the elimination of impurities. Both the spiritual and material worlds are also regulated by the law that prescribes the order of things in the universe, as well as God's original purpose for each one, animate and inanimate.

Growing Purity

To our limited human perception, the realm of spirit contains many mysteries. As mortal creatures, we may never uncover them all, but certain things are becoming clear. First, the time lag between spiritual changes and their repercussions in the realm of matter is now considerably less than it used to be. Second, as the power of purification grows stronger, Johrei is increasingly more effective. These tendencies are a direct result of a shift in the spiritual world, which is growing brighter as earthly paradise comes closer.

We also know now that certain forces endowed with purificatory energy radiate from the realm of spirit.

They support all birth and growth; they propel the purification process. The spiritual world is becoming brighter because the strength of these forces is increasing. Although we cannot yet analyze or even identify such spiritual forces, what is important is our recognition that they exist and are basic to the truth of nature and reality.

In all history, few individuals have attained a state wherein they were aware of the full reality of the realm of spirit. The souls of those few reached high levels on the spiritual ladder. This rising spiritual progression has three main strata, each of which is again divided into three. The soul of every person, depending on its purity, takes a place in one of the nine levels, but it is possible to ascend or descend from any given level in accordance with the depth of one's faith and the quality of his ideas, words, and conduct. The souls of those who have attained the state of greatest purity are elevated to the highest rank.

Upon death of the body, God judges the soul of each individual.* Only those that reach heaven, which is the uppermost level on the spiritual ladder, shall see God. Souls which enter the middle strata are purified further before they are permitted to rise. On the lower levels reside souls under punishment for disbelief or other major sins committed in this world.

God wills that we elevate our earthly civilization to a higher plane. The new civilization, while remaining of this world, will be a genuine manifestation of divine

* See p. 82 for further discussions on the meaning of death and the life of the soul after death.—Eds.

44

providence, premised on the fulfillment of God's will for man. Insofar as man, under the supervision of God, is the executor in building the new civilization—the carpenter, so to speak—he must grow spiritually, and his soul must rise on the spiritual ladder if he is to perform that crucial task. Let us turn to man as a spiritual entity, focusing on the working of the soul, the agent of human elevation.

MAN'S SPIRITUAL BEING

Through the centuries it has usually been far more difficult to explain evil than good, partly because good does not demand rationalization. Evil itself can never be justified, no matter how one tries to explain it, but at least it can be understood, if only partially, especially if we begin by describing the whole spiritual make-up of a human being.

First of all, the human entity is both physical and spiritual and the two aspects are closely integrated, but it is possible to examine the spirit alone and consider its structure in terms of three distinct levels. The soul, the agency through which God works in man, is at the apex. The heart lies in the middle, and at the base is the spiritual body system (the spiritual or immaterial body), which controls the physical body system according to the law of spiritual precedence over the material.

Receptor of the Divine Voice

The spirit may also be conceived in terms of concentric circles, as illustrated below. Created to receive

45

God's will for the whole person, the soul is the innermost core. It is enclosed by the heart, which receives orders from it and so becomes, figuratively, a workplace for the soul. The heart is also the locus of any conflict between conscience and evil influences in the individual. The spiritual body system, on the other hand, envelops both the soul and the heart and pervades the physical system. It takes a shape identical to the physical body, while remaining imperceptible to the senses and impossible to identify by scientific means.

The formation of a human being begins with conception. Conception is the physical joining of a male spermatozoon with the female ovum, but spiritually it is the creation in this world of an individual soul equipped with

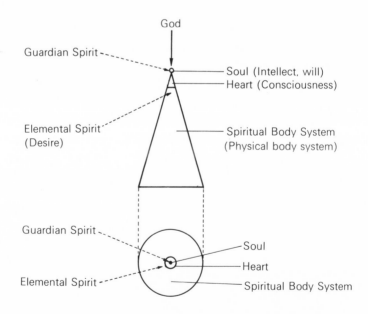

a strong will to love God and one's fellow humans, as well as the power of intellect to know the particular mission assigned to the person by God. Insofar as the soul is the direct receptor of God's will, it is essentially good, and strong against evil.* When Mencius said, "Man is good by nature," he was talking about the soul as the seat of conscience. One's conscience "aches" when the divine message is in the form of a reprimand or rebuke. Faith, good will, compassion, reason, and so on are all attributes of the soul.

Each individual has the freedom of will to follow God's path or go astray, to choose good or evil. Ultimately, the soul must decide which, and that choice determines the overall spiritual state of the person. When the soul is pure, it is attuned only to the voice of God; it always distinguishes correctly between good and evil, and it chooses good.

The heart is the domain of consciousness. Operative in it are both the dictates of "reason" from the soul and demands from what we call the elemental spirit, the source of human desires. If the soul is impure, the elemental spirit can more easily fill the heart with immoderate, inflated desires that counter the will of God. All our wishes are registered in the heart and are screened there for action, and so when the heart is swayed by evil it inclines one towards destruction and harm. When the heart is firmly under the control of good, it motivates constructive efforts and selfless acts to help others.

* In actuality, regardless of its essential goodness, the soul in most people is vulnerable to evil influences, as discussed on p. 52.—Eds.

The spiritual body system has no autonomous will, since it mainly provides a nexus for the soul and the heart. The state of the soul, however, is clearly reflected upon the spiritual body system through the heart, and in turn upon the physical body system. The immaterial body is adversely affected by any acts violating the spiritual laws that govern all creation.

Control of Desires

Whereas the soul is the seat of man's conscience, the elemental spirit is the source of the basic desires necessary for his life in this world. The human desires include physical impulses, the urge for intellectual, emotional, and esthetic satisfaction, and the wish for material possessions and social recognition, among others. Desires are by no means evil in themselves, for without them we would lack the compulsion from some of the primary forces that enable human life to continue. But desires left to rage with abandon drain one of constructive energy and drag him down into a subhuman state where neither the heart nor soul has any control. A person in that state is no longer able to fulfill the wonder of being human.

If one examines his feelings carefully, he often senses conflict in his heart between inordinate desire and his conscience. Man is made to have the power to control his desires and follow his conscience; as long as the soul dominates the heart and keeps the elemental spirit in check, a person's life will not deviate very far from the will of God. But if the dedication to abide faithfully by

God's will and fulfill the mission He bestowed falters, the soul itself loses its authority over the elemental spirit, and manifestations of evil in thoughts and behavior increase.

It is possible to recognize when the elemental spirit has grown too powerful; it causes a person to grow preoccupied with vanity, jealousy, or prejudice. Many times he becomes so involved with pleasures and luxury that he thinks of no one's well-being but his own. An inflated elemental spirit can also lure a person to seek tyrannical power over others, to monopolize wealth or knowledge, or to harm others by theft, fraud, violence, or any of the many other ways people find to hurt each other.

Depending on how far the soul is open to God's voice, hence how completely it controls the elemental spirit, human life can range between godliness and uncontrolled animality. Virtuous, we move closer to God, but dominated by desires, we plunge into a state where we can no longer make a distinction between good and evil. We must never try to crush our basic desires completely, even if we could, for they help us to live. But we must not let them grow beyond moderation to a point where the voice of conscience is no longer heard.

The Guardian Spirit

To assist in controlling the elemental spirit, the guardian spirit comes to attend the soul soon after a person's birth. The guardian spirit abides with the person as his protector, staying with him until death. Unlike the evil-prone elemental spirit, the guardian spirit is always good, and tries to warn one of calamity, mishap, wrong-doing, negligence, degrading influences, and all else that might endanger him. We hear of people having premonitions, ominous dreams, or unexpected obstacles coming across their path. Sometimes we find a person at cross-purposes when things do not go smoothly. These phenomena are often the work of the guardian spirit. By missing a train, for example, someone is saved from an accident; he is tempted to cheat or steal, and something unexpected intervenes to stop him. The guardian spirit causes such occurrences to prevent harm and misfortune, and also positively encourages righteousness at all times, so that wrongdoing and involvement in potentially harm-ful affairs cannot occur. The guardian spirit's power to resist evil forces ultimately is commensurate with the purity of the soul under its charge.

Lest a person be overpowered by evil influences, his guardian spirit helps develop the good character and ability distinctive to that person. In so doing, the guardian spirit is assisting in God's plan for the world. Even then, the guardian spirit must sometimes cause a person to suffer in order to discipline and refine his soul. How hard one is disciplined and how great the affliction depends on the gravity of the individual mission—the more momentous one's mission, the more one suffers.

Besides the elemental spirit and the guardian spirit, other spirits are sometimes present. These are so-called alien spirits, and they can possess a person whose spiritual purity has deteriorated too far. Unbelievers, even those whose behavior is kind and helpful, are precariously vulnerable to possession at any time. Those who were possessed by these evil spirits abound among the many tyrants and dictators in history. What conditions lead to possession by an alien spirit, and what does "spiritual impurity" mean? To answer these questions, we must talk about sin and what we call "clouds" that form in the human spirit.

HUMAN RESPONSIBILITY

Faith is our only assurance of salvation, and only by faith can we fully accept God's providence. We must keep it strong. To help us in our faith God has given us signs that He ordains the reign of evil to give way to a new and blessed existence for man. We have much to thank God for in the certainty of a better world to come. But while we thank Him for the promise of a better future, how should we interpret the past? Should we place our suffering on God's shoulders, passing on to Him the blame for all our miseries until now? What kind of providence is it that made the whole human race suffer for so long? Why were we rendered so vulnerable to evil that we almost exterminated ourselves?

Origin of Unhappiness

We must not make the mistake of blaming providence when we search for answers to these questions, for it was man's choice that determined the human condition through the ages. Man originally created his own un-happiness by refusing to heed God's will.* In willfully alienating themselves from God, people emasculated the power of good and let evil grow. As they continued to defy divine law, their misery increased. Even then, few sought reconciliation with God.

Let us look more carefully at the consequences of the refusal to follow God's commandments, and let us also examine the reasons for our increasing vulnerability and unhappiness. When man sinned for the first time, the capacity of his soul to respond to God's will began to degenerate. As he deviated further from the divine path, his soul became increasingly less attuned to the voice of God, intensifying the proclivity to sin. With man's fall from grace, spiritual impurities also began to collect on the soul. Figuratively called "clouds," these impurities grew thicker through the generations, making people that much more open to evil influences. Clouds also have undermined man's understanding of the spiritual laws governing creation.

As we have noted, the soul is responsible for the spiritual state of a person. Souls free from sin are receptive to the divine will; unclouded, they have a protective, luminous quality that repels evil spirits. Those who try hard to follow in God's path are less prone to wrongdoing than those with little or no faith, and their souls tend to be purer and better able to combat evil. Clouds generated on the soul as a result of sin dim its luminous quality, which in turn gives easier access for alien spirits to possess

* This is explained further on pp. 57–58, and 78–79.—Eds.

a person. Thus a heavily clouded soul is a likely candidate for possession. At the very least, it is led easily into sin.

Clouds on the soul are projected throughout the human spirit, thereby making both the heart and the spiritual body system more vulnerable. Clouds in the heart may invite an alien spirit to possess this vital area in the spiritual make-up. When the heart is beclouded, moreover, the elemental spirit becomes strong, often to the point where the soul is unable to control it, and the potential for wrongdoing grows. Since clouds provide a comfortable habitat, their presence in the spiritual body system robs it of the strength to ward off possession by evil spirits. Besides being affected by clouds projected from the soul, the immaterial body is also contaminated directly in the act of violating a spiritual law.

A Way to Begin

Most people today are so sinful that their souls are heavily clouded, providing wide latitude for the work of harmful spirits. That is one reason we are seeing the spread of crime and implacable hatred among people. Because the state of society fundamentally depends on the spiritual state of its individual members, our world will become a better place to live in only as the clouds are lifted from more and more souls. But most of our leaders do not know the real source of crime, antisocial acts, or harmful deviance, and so they try to repress such behavior by legal, coercive, or other stopgap measures. These methods are not really effective because they do nothing to dispel the clouds on the human soul or help restore its luminous power. Hence they can neither combat evil successfully nor resolve the afflictions of man and society.

Sin is remitted by divine absolution alone. When clouds have formed on the soul as a consequence of sin, the only way to set about eradicating them is by asking forgiveness from God. Clouds on the soul are actually very difficult to dispel, but in His great love, God has given us the divine light of Johrei as a way to begin. Literally a method of spiritual purification, Johrei efficiently dispels clouds that have accumulated in the spiritual body system. The cleansing and healing power of Johrei often has the long-term effect of leading those who receive it to repent of their sins. Recipients grow in righteousness and goodness, and their faith in God is awakened, renewed, and deepened. Its administrators, too, as they see the blessings of Johrei appear before their own eyes and directly witness God's unfathomable power and love, experience a deepening of faith. As faith grows, clouds on the soul decrease, bringing the person closer to fulfilling God's will.

Why has God ordained that we begin practicing Johrei throughout the world only now, at this point in history? This problem is closely related to His judgment. Soon after man entered the world, he let moral evil into the world, also. The struggle in human communities to undo that great wrong and to preserve the good and keep it strong has helped the advance of material civilization, but while it was being waged, evil grew too powerful. If evil were unrestrained and allowed to dominate our world completely, humanity itself would be in mortal peril. But God is not going to let us keep groping in ignorance. He wills that evil be reined in and civilization transformed. By giving us the power of Johrei, He is reaching out to help us find reconciliation with Him. He is giving us support for our own efforts to renew our faith in Him and let the divine light purify our bodies, our souls, and our world. We have no other choice but to respond to God's call to us to fulfill our task, using Johrei as a spiritual vehicle to carry us towards awakening and repentance.

2

Realization of Human Hope

Torch Bearers

VIRTUALLY all the many religions that have arisen at one time or another have defined and pursued some version of good while seeking the means to eliminate what they perceive as evil. All the great religions share basically similar concepts of moral evil and extol benevolence, compassion, or love. But how can God be infinite love, if in His world people are tortured by evil forces? If God truly loved us, would He not have spared us those trials?

Great Religions

The wonder of God's works begins to become clear only when we understand His original intent for man. God created man to be free, to be able to follow in His path on his own volition and to reach a state of godliness so that he may participate in His eternal life. That very freedom, however, offered man the opposite choice also—to deviate from God's path and degenerate to a state of animality. When man first contravened God's will, his soul grew clouded and he could no longer clearly hear what God was communicating. This was the phase in the story of man when he brought in moral evil and became vulnerable to it, and sin then became pervasive in human society. What is so hard to understand here is that God did not choose to let evil forces scourge the earth just to punish; He let them remain so that the tortures of their presence might encourage people to repent and gladly return to His path. How much more difficult it is to appreciate, therefore, His infinite mercy in lightening man's trials by turning the effects of evil into occasions for good.*

Although many forms of evil are allowed to persist, they have never been completely free to range wantonly through the world. Throughout history evil forces have been limited; otherwise, the human race would have been decimated long ago. It would have been impossible to accomplish anything or work with a sense of security, or to achieve even a semblance of peace in life. The world could easily have become a place of demons and orderless, destructive chaos.

The rise of religions partially answered the need to control the moral evil that man let loose on himself. One of the most significant was Christianity. In contrast to Sakyamuni's teachings, which are based on the hope of personal spiritual enlightenment or absolute peace of mind through meditation, Jesus' teachings emphasize salvation for humankind, which is postulated on a personal relationship of love for God and other people. In that it

* This paradox is explained on pp. 39–40.—Eds.

stresses the oneness of the human community, Christianity is of and in this world. The doctrine of love for God and man became a powerful agent in the regulation and control of evil. Those who were strengthened by love through their faith were better able to withstand sin, evil, and suffering, and that gave the religion its main impetus.

Thus, even though evil forces have continued to torment and taunt man, slowly over the centuries the great religions have prepared people for the time when those forces will retreat before the stronger power of good. Several major religions, in particular, have assumed a crucial role in guiding their followers according to the divine will. Jesus was called the Redeemer, who atoned for the sins of all, so that we might be saved. On behalf of all people, he asked for forgiveness from God. His act of supreme love brought light and warmth to an unhappy world. Sakyamuni also devoted his life to helping in the search for human salvation. It took many long years of meditating for Sakyamuni to understand his true mission and for his teaching to crystallize. Then, as one of the Buddhist sutras asserts, he had a vision of the world of Maitreya-bodhisattva thousands of years ahead in the future.

Catalytic Experience

Many centuries later, most of us in the modern world find ourselves still unable to repent and return to God's path. Our refusal to repent seems to have stymied goodness even further. It has brought us widespread hunger and oppression, rising crime and corruption, more deadly uses of chemicals and drugs, the destruction of nature, the threat of nuclear war, and above all, the spread of unbelief and atheism. Now, in our time, the human condition is ripe for us to answer God's call for repentance and to fulfill His will so that at last we may find happiness on earth.

The very act of repentance, besides the effect it has on the spirit, generates a change in the totality of one's thinking patterns. One becomes capable of a new level of perception and can use with compassion the knowledge our civilization has accumulated, to help the human race. Sometimes, conversely, an intellectually shattering experience prompts a person to repent, upon which his attitudes undergo further, profound change. Johrei is one such experience, and at long last it is spreading to bring blessings that defy standard explanations. It guides us to faith in God and sets us to the task of fashioning a world in which evil, sin, and suffering will diminish.

Of course for those who cannot pull away and place the material in its proper perspective, it is hard to understand why anyone should embrace God now. Their reluctance poses a difficult challenge. But God will no longer tolerate unbelief. It must be overcome, for it is too great an impediment to the unfolding of His plan. It is time for those who do not yet believe in God to awaken quickly, for if they do not, their unbelief will doom them to destruction. The great change has come when good will triumph. Those who try to obstruct the divine work during the period of change will not survive God's wrath.

They still have a chance now, however, and can take the way that God has opened.

Good will prevail when we begin to follow the divine will and control evil desires in our hearts. We will see wars break out rarely, the hungry being fed, and the sick being cured. So far there has been little choice but to move forward on the basis of the knowledge that was available, and scientists have done their best. They have done so well, in fact, that the job of changing attitudes towards science and technology and reorienting popular thinking is very difficult, but that is one of the crucial tasks that lie before us now: to encourage others to repent and let God's knowledge guide all human endeavor.

From Night to Day

Sakyamuni described this world variously as an "impure land," a "burning house where sentient beings live," and as a place of suffering. He went on to classify human suffering as being of four types: birth, old age, sickness, and death. From the moment of birth, a person is destined to endure endless misery, unable to escape the painful burden. In the darkness it is useless to sustain any great hope. There can be no peace of mind, for no one knows what fate may befall him at any moment. Our provisional world renders everything nonsubstantial in the end. Nothing can be eternal, no matter how we labor to create permanence. All human desire is illusory, temporary, and relative. We have no choice but to accept our painful destiny in this world, and rather than struggling to escape, we should seek spiritual enlightenment in order to attain ultimate peace.

Causal Relationship

What Sakyamuni thought of as "this world" we call the Age of Night, the long stretch of human history during which evil forces have been allowed wide limits, while people reap the consequences of departing from God's path. During the Age of Night people suffer from sickness, poverty, and strife because of heavy clouds in their spirit. Now, however, a period of transition has begun that will carry the world from the Age of Night to a completely new era, the Age of Day.

When the transition started, the realm of spirit, where the great change originates, imperceptibly brightened. With the approaching Age of Day it grows lighter and warmer, and the purifying power* that springs from it is also growing stronger, in order to cleanse the spiritual world of its impurities—the clouds. As we have seen, clouds collect in the realm of spirit as a result of our transgressions of God's will and the spiritual laws of nature. Purification—dispelling of the clouds—is usually accompanied by some form of human suffering or other. During the Age of Night, however, purificatory action in the spiritual realm reverberates in the material realm with a considerable time lag, making it difficult for people to see the direct causal relationship between their wrongdoing and suffering. Primarily because of the

---

* The purificatory energy emanating from the realm of spirit is explained on pp. 43–44.—Eds.

heavy clouds on their souls, and secondarily because of delayed repercussions, people in the Age of Night tend to seek immediate, albeit temporary, gains or results, even if it means going against the will of God and the spiritual laws governing this world. The consequence is a spiral increase of both clouds on the soul and suffering. If we cannot stop this vicious circle, it will destroy human civilization and wipe out our species, laying waste to all of nature at the same time.

With the approach of the Age of Day, the time lag between change in the realm of spirit and its reverberations in the realm of matter is diminishing. That means that any purifying action in the spiritual world is reflected faster in the material world. Hence, people are growing increasingly sensitive to the causal relationship between their thought or behavior and the suffering it may cause. From now on, it will become more and more difficult to act in defiance of God's will and the spiritual laws, even for temporary, immediate gains or results.

As Night becomes Day, it will be next to impossible for any nation to achieve its territorial or other ambitions through war or invasion. Unjust or exploitive means will serve less and less profitably those who seek to amass wealth. Any attempt to satisfy one's desires at the expense of other people's interests will prove to be futile. Artificial methods that run counter to the spiritual laws of nature will become exceedingly ineffectual in all areas of human endeavor. All in all, the stronger purificatory power of the spiritual realm will inhibit us from committing evil acts as the new Age of Day draws near. Conditions conducive to repentance will then prevail in this world.

Great Transformation

Right now, we are living through a momentous event in the universe. Our world is on the verge of transformation, for the great purifying action that has been set in motion in the spiritual realm will soon reverberate in this world—it will be a global upheaval. That upheaval will cleanse everyone in both body and spirit. Those who repent and are forgiven will survive to enter the Age of Day and join the new world of true happiness, free from suffering.

When the change began, it was so gradual that we did not notice, for we could not perceive the spiritual realities. But we must be always receptive to even the subtlest signs of change taking place in the realm of spirit. We must use the chance as it comes and repent. One of the most important visible signs of change in our world is the growing effectiveness of Johrei in curing people with serious afflictions. The many testimonies of personal experience with Johrei offer heart-warming, joyful proof of its truth. They relate how the blessings of Johrei have awakened person after person to the existence of God. When someone repents of his lack of belief, finds the love of God, and learns to lead a truly human life that conforms with the divine will, he begins genuinely to feel the presence of God. Many, many people have experienced this process of religious conversion and have fully embraced God since coming in contact with Johrei. The purifying power from the realm of spirit is growing stronger, and at the same time, in the realm of matter, artificial means to suppress purification are becoming increasingly less effective. Today Johrei works for even the most stubborn unbeliever, cleansing his spiritual body system and helping to awaken him to the existence of God and His way.

Misery and suffering need no longer be endured. If we open our eyes to the truth, we can begin to overcome old beliefs and realize the true civilization. God will not wait much longer to see that man at last follows His will. When the judgment comes, the age of darkness will end.* Our mission now is to tell all people of God's work and what is to come. Our great, inevitable task of redirecting human life is the first step towards the realization of true civilization.

JOHREI AND AWAKENING

In the progress of history we see the unfolding of God's providence. It has been a long process of preparation and change in the Age of Night leading towards the Age of Day. During the Age of Night people brought forth misery for themselves by letting evil run rampant—all because they deviated from the path of God. Evil continues to dominate history because so few have truly unshakable faith in God, much less in His work. Many of us still doubt or even deny God's being, but disbe-

* See Commentary, "Faith," p. 195.—Eds.

65

lief is one of the most dreadful of sins. It has warped the nature of scientific and technological progress, encouraging heavily materialistic tendencies and pushing humankind to the brink of self-annihilation.

Gift for Humankind

Now, however, as the transition to the Age of Day advances, our world is approaching a great spiritual upheaval. If we are to survive the historic transition and save our civilization from irretrievable destruction, we must repent and return to God's path. We must respond of our own will to the call from God and join in the task of building Paradise on Earth. If we cannot build an earthly paradise, our hope of salvation, too, will be lost.

Johrei is a divine gift bestowed on all, to prepare us for the imminent spiritual upheaval and participation in building earthly paradise. It is one way God shows His love for us and demonstrates His wish to awaken our souls and save us from self-destruction. Johrei already is being practiced, but only on a very small scale. When many more people accept it and their souls wake to the existence of God, human history will actually become the record of growing happiness and deepening spirituality.

When the divine light is transmitted through the hand of the Johrei administrator, it begins to change and strengthen the receiver. Because it cleanses the spiritual body system of clouds, Johrei heals any spiritual or physical ailment, including diseases thought to be incurable or terminal. The blessings made possible by Johrei offer to even the most determined unbeliever proof of the truth of God and the absolute certainty of His grace. In its intrinsic meaning, then, Johrei is a way to help a person to repent and to experience the joy of deepening faith.

Johrei is not the only way to encourage repentance, but it affects even the most sinful souls. Admittedly, there are exceptional cases when people fail to go very far in spiritual awakening. Whether or not a person will truly repent and embrace God's love is basically the decision of his soul, and the outcome depends on how sincerely he seeks personal union with Him. But, in dispelling the clouds in the spiritual body system and demonstrating, by its miraculous healing power, God's blessings, Johrei can and does create a condition within us that is conducive to repentance and faith in God. Those who receive Johrei and feel genuine repentance will be purified in their souls, and they will find their love of God and fellow humans growing stronger.

Process of Conversion

Again and again we have seen instances when the souls of the administrator and the receiver alike were purified and both people were more fully awakened to the truth of God. Johrei actually prompts one to pray; it enables him to concentrate better and to have deeper sincerity in prayer. Thus it also encourages one to try to understand the divine will and to live a better life, to grow morally and spiritually. One experiences what is actually a conversion. Nonetheless, the process leading to that stage is by no means smooth or easy. Many undergo painful internal struggles, torn between the lure of atheism and the divine voices of conscience, or between their old notions and new beliefs. For many, the process necessitates a revolutionary change in their entire outlook on life and the world, and the replacement of old values with new. It is very difficult for all of us to travel the long distance between an initial, superficial acceptance of God's being and a deep personal relationship with Him. It is even more difficult to leap from mere private satisfaction and peace of mind to a higher plane of faith beyond reasoning, where one can identify himself with the whole of mankind and live in accord with God's will.

Anyone can receive Johrei, regardless of creed, race, or nationality, and can be healed by it, even if he is suspicious or antagonistic at first. Yet the effectiveness fades if he continues to receive Johrei and in spite of blessings that come to him, including the chance to be led to repentance, still doubts God's love and fails to follow His will.* Likewise, once he learns how, anyone can administer Johrei, which is neither arduous nor difficult. But there are individual differences in the power it exerts, for both administrator and receiver, depending essentially on the depth of faith.

Johrei is best administered by someone with deep faith. He or she begins by making a prayer to God in an appropriately solemn or quiet environment. The long-term benefits of Johrei are commensurate with the depth of the administrator's faith, and also with his sincerity

* Such a believer will eventually cease to receive God's grace altogether, unless he repents. See Commentary, "Faith," p. 195.—Eds.

and acceptance of God's love. That is why Johrei is most effective when it is given by one whose soul is relatively unclouded and who lives the faith he really feels. The purer and stronger the soul, the greater the blessings that Johrei will bring.

Sign of Forgiveness

In administering Johrei, one becomes the instrument of God, a transmitter of divine light through prayers to the Creator. Therefore, if a person gives Johrei with an attitude of pride, or in the self-confident anticipation of "the results," or if he feels some kind of self-satisfaction at having achieved "results" himself, the power of the divine light will diminish radically.

Many people who receive divine blessings through Johrei nevertheless go astray, without experiencing conversion, either because of their ungrateful failure to embrace God or their sinful idolization of themselves. But many, many more, filled with respect, even awe, as they witness and are moved by the unfathomable greatness of God's mercy, choose to turn to Him. They begin with good works, most notably sharing the power of Johrei with the afflicted and helping them to spiritually perceive the presence of God. After a long, painful process of internalization, in which meditation and prayer also play an important role, some finally undergo total conversion and begin a life of genuine penitence. It is at this point that a person's soul begins to be purified as he receives forgiveness and can at last overcome his sinfulness.

There have been many instances of conversion at the

point of death when a person finally grasps the enormity of his sins and repents. Johrei's purifying power and personal repentance together enable the dying to repose in peace, assured of God's forgiveness. Sometimes a person receives a life-giving flow of spiritual strength at the last minute and he is saved from death. It is at such times that the drama and power of God's mercy are literally miraculous. The effect is the emergence of a new and ever-growing determination to follow in God's path. From then on the power of Johrei, as one channels and receives it, grows steadily stronger and one moves further and deeper in understanding of and accord with God's will.

The gift of Johrei should be understood as an indication of how much God is trying to help us. Accepting that with gratitude, we can take hope that our world will change if we wish it, and we must try sincerely to live as close to Him as we can. We must make unending efforts to let goodness grow in our hearts and guard against evil. We must also try to make others happy and bring them joy, always thanking God in His mercy. God will purify the souls of those who make that effort and try to fulfill their mission on earth.

Johrei is but one way of helping people to gain and strengthen their faith in God, yet it is a sure sign that our sins are to be forgiven and Paradise on Earth is drawing near. God has given each of us this means to change our lives and world and achieve true health in body and spirit, in preparation for the new phase of human history that will unfold in Paradise on Earth.

World of Perfect Harmony

When God revealed Johrei, He gave us a concrete, undeniable sign that the promise of salvation ultimately would be fulfilled. Johrei embodies God's word that a balance in our civilization will be achieved, righting the ancient disorder, and that we in our earthly existence will see our lives transformed to a state of happiness, security, goodness, and peace. Johrei conveys to us the truth that salvation, the goal towards which the soul is essentially directed, can be attained. Thus, while bringing relief from physical and spiritual distress, Johrei encourages us to participate in the metamorphosis of our civilization.

Just as man was never a passive vessel in history, from henceforth also he is to be a creative agent of God in the new civilization. As people begin to adjust their ways of life in accord with that task, they will be venturing into the realization of their full humanity and at the same time bringing balance to the fabric of civilization itself.

The Twain Shall Meet

If we look briefly at world culture to review how it has taken shape, we can make a basic distinction between Eastern and Western cultures and identify certain characteristics in each. At the risk of over-generalization, we may say that Eastern culture is built on certain "vertical" principles that govern ethics and social relations. The stress on loyalty to one's lord or master, filial piety, respect for seniority, and group solidarity centered around a symbol of paternal authority are all characteristic of the vertical orientation of Eastern culture. By contrast, Western culture, where the equality of all individuals before the absolute, transcendental God is emphasized more heavily, is characterized by "horizontal" principles. The Christian concept of love for all people—marital and family love, and love for one's neighbors—symbolizes the horizontal orientation of Western culture. This is what propelled the dynamic extension of European civilization through different countries and societies.

The civilization that grew up in the West was meant to provide a universal vehicle for the realization of the divine plan in all lands and among all people, and a channel for the development of individualism and rationalism. It was no coincidence that the scientific way of thinking matured in the context of the Christian ethos, which provided the foundation for modern industrial society. By contrast, the vertical, particularistic orientation of Eastern culture laid more stress on the unity of the group—the family, community, domain, and nation— than the inalienable rights of the individual. Collective interests and self-deprecation were valued above self-assertion and individual growth and happiness.

What happened, however, was that Eastern and Western cultures tended to go too far in their respective orientations. They became either too heavily group-oriented or overly individualistic and rationalistic. As a result the equilibrium of the two premises was destroyed not only within each, but in the very meeting of world cultures. The chaos that prevails is the consequence. God ordains that in the building of earthly paradise, a balanced fusion of the Eastern and Western principles be achieved, bringing horizontal and vertical together into perfect harmony.

Beyond Prejudice

Perfect harmony combined with its correlative, infinite flexibility, will characterize the new global civilization. Together they will allow limitless freedom to develop the human culture in either direction. The principle of a free and flexible fusion of the spiritual and the material will then govern the creative and intellectual life of the individual in earthly paradise. Truth is never wholly spiritual nor wholly material; it is both. So it is with Johrei, which incorporates both religious and scientific truths. Thus, Johrei symbolizes the perfect balance and flexibility characteristic of the civilization to come. It is this integrative quality of Johrei that makes it universally applicable and accessible to anyone, even those who have long ignored God and rejected the spiritual world.

We should always think and behave according to common sense, faithful to our true emotions, not momentary passions. This is precisely why our faith attaches such overriding importance to common sense, moderation, and balanced thinking and behavior. It is unfortunate that good sense is often scorned as lack of imagination and biased judgment misread as a mark of greatness, for history shows that prejudice is the harbinger of failure. In any case, the person who is unable or unwilling to restrain biases in his thought and actions will most likely never achieve anything but notoriety. True greatness is measured by a person's contribution to the new civilization, through the fulfillment of the mission given him by God. The first part of the individual's task is, therefore, to find the right balance within himself so that he may apply it to his society.

In the world of perfect harmony, acts of aggression will be extremely uncommon because the motivation for such behavior will disappear. Daily life and activities will be governed increasingly by the principle of fairness and will be guided by a growing sense of true justice that enables people to transcend narrow, partisan interests. Human relations will enter a wholly new phase, because the discrepancies of power among and between individuals and groups will diminish as their materialistic desires decrease.

Penal and criminal laws are necessary to restrain the conduct of wicked or misguided people, but in the new world, where evil will steadily fade and people will be rarely motivated by base desires, a system of strict laws will become increasingly less relevant. Conflicts of interest will dwindle until finally all struggles arising out of ambition, even out of bad judgment, will cease. Disputes will be resolved peacefully, just as population imbalances, unequal distribution of resources and wealth, and other inequities will be adjusted with fairness and justice.

Those who are overburdened with sin and are incapable of accepting God's grace will not survive to participate in the new civilization. Earthly paradise will be built by those who have repented and received God's forgiveness, people strong enough to be able to withstand evil and use all the strength they have in carrying out the particular mission God assigned each one. Those people will have survived His judgment, to know undreamed of happiness.

REWARDS OF PENITENCE

The true civilization will be a Paradise on Earth built by the faithful in obedience to God's will. It will be an ideal world of truth, goodness, and beauty, but only those who survive God's judgment will witness its completion.

Paradise in Our Hearts

Before we can begin the monumental task of transforming this world, however, we must each build a paradise in our own hearts. We must repent of our sins and embrace unqualified faith in God. Genuine repentance involves much more than regular church attendance and good behavior; it means a life of total commitment to God and enduring, unselfish love for our fellow humans.

The purity and goodness of our thoughts, what we keep in our hearts and minds, give goodness to our words and deeds. A constant and conscious effort to eradicate evil thoughts and overcome self-righteousness is the premise of a life of repentance, and freedom from egotism is a prerequisite for genuine altruism. If we can permanently overcome self-centeredness in our thinking and behavior, and liberate ourselves from the fetters of the need for personal gratification, then we are ready for the most important step—to leave everything to God in faith, while making the effort to understand His will.* It is not the opinions of others or our own mundane inclinations, but God's will that must guide our daily living. When His will becomes our goal, we will naturally direct our total being towards its fulfillment.

Faith as strong as that can stand up against threats, persecution, suffering or condemnation, and it opens horizons for a whole new way of living. People who have such faith let God's will direct everything they do, and they are filled with constant, grateful awareness that God gives them everything they have, starting with life itself.

If our faith is firm, we recognize that complaining and despair lead only away from God, and that even suffering is to be accepted, for it has its own rewards from God. Can we reject the hand that tries to help? Should we not, rather, welcome pain when this in itself is a form of purification, a chance to make us into better people? Should we not love God so much that we can thank Him for this, too? For the providence of God transcends human understanding. Suffering, indeed, is often the first step on the road to salvation.

If we truly love God, we love other people and place their happiness above our own. Loving God is to be willing to risk unhappiness, misery, even hell for ourselves for the sake of someone else. That means helping people and leading them away from sin and teaching

* See Commentary, "Wisdom," p. 212.—Eds.

them of God's mercy, with the belief in His almighty goodness and the universal brotherhood of man. To transmit the light of Johrei and lead others to faith in God is one of the most powerful expressions of love there is. And our faith is rooted first and foremost in love.

God honors a person of faithfulness, just as He helps one of true strength. If we wish God to support us, we must be absolutely faithful to Him, to His law and commandments. Then we must be true to ourselves, to our conscience and commitments. Faithfulness must also govern all social relations between individuals, between organizations, communities, and nations. A person of true strength has the courage to seek and overcome evils within, resisting all temptation to be unjust, dishonest, or malicious. He never gives in to greed or self-indulgence, and he can temper his passions. It is not easy to acquire such strength. The person must have firm determination to combat evil and give sincere prayers for divine protection. Only then, with the grace of God, will his soul be able to resist evil.

Trials of Faith

God sometimes puts the faithful through trials, to test the strength of their belief in Him. If they can meet these trials successfully, they will be given even greater missions to perform in their lives. For example, the faithful may encounter events which, through no fault of their own, seriously threaten their social, economic, or even spiritual well-being. They must endure such events with humility, without hostility or resentment. Such times are an opportunity God gives them to elevate their faith to a still higher plane, and for that reason they should be met with gratitude.

Sometimes things do not go as expected or planned, even when we try our best to live in accord with God's will as we perceive it. Either our intent contravenes God's will, or it is still premature in terms of God's plan for us. Thus, whatever happens in our lives is ultimately governed by the providence of God. To assume that what we believe is *always* correct and act on the basis of that self-righteous assumption invariably induces a betrayal of God's will. Arrogance and self-conceit make us vulnerable to the lures and temptations of evil spirits, no matter how devoted we think we are to our faith. Seeking forgiveness, we must open ourselves to God's grace so that we may become His instrument Only by realizing how imperfect and sinful we are, can we make humility and obedience the guiding principles in our lives.

Each of us is destined at birth to bear the legacy of man's first and continuing rebellion against God. That legacy is the tendency to sin. A person sins when he succumbs to the inclination to contravene the divine will by pursuing inordinate desires. It is an inclination that lurks in the hearts of all people whether they believe in God or not, but many are not even aware of it. Unless a person has a deep and perceptive faith, he will not be able to discern that tendency within, and he may be unable to control it. The danger is that it can render him deaf to the voices of his conscience and to the divine inspirations sent to the soul, and cause him to subvert God's admonitions. That person becomes further and further alienated from God in an age-old repetition of the first time man turned from Him to worship the profane.

When one considers that we cannot sustain ourselves even one day without God's grace, each of us is only a trifling existence in the universe. It is impossible for us fully to understand God, or to judge all that is good or evil and pass absolute judgment on others. We must, therefore, live a life of faith and always be obedient to His will. We must place ourselves under His benevolent command, living fully in love by His grace. In the sense that we are capable of all that if we wish, we are, each of us, also profoundly important in the eyes of God.

The deeper our faith, the more fundamentally we realize the gravity of our sins and the magnificent vastness of God's love. That realization alone can awaken the soul to true repentance, but in the process we must keep God always in our thoughts and never stop praying for divine grace and for the power to follow Him in daily life.

If we receive Johrei with sincere prayers for His help, God will send forth ever stronger light to dispel the clouds on our souls. Thus Johrei is a sign of God's forgiveness and, by extension, of the imminent happiness in Paradise on Earth.

Paradise on Earth

People who survive the divine judgment will enter a whole new mode of existence in Paradise on Earth. As their sins are remitted, day by day their souls will be purer and less clouded. They will also grow wiser as they become better able to judge how God wishes them to conduct themselves in the new world. Each person will know God's will for him and learn to live by it.

Pervasive Beauty

In the coming age, good will prevail over evil, for only those in whom good reigns supreme will survive, and any elements of animality that remain in the spirit of man will be effectively controlled. All people will be moved to seek peace above all and to shun conflict. They will become more and more sensitive to the ugly qualities of evil and malice in their hearts, and they will try harder to replace them with good and compassion. This, then, is the time of the restoration of man's full humanity, as his soul grows pure in the love of God.

If exposure to the truth inspires an intellectual awakening to the need for repentance, then exposure to beauty and empathy with it help arouse and lead the soul to search out truth and goodness. That universal search will result in an earthly paradise so filled with inexpressible loveliness—of which we have only hints at present in nature and in man's creations—that it will be a world that embodies beauty itself.

Even during the Age of Night, beauty has had a very special role to play in guiding the spiritual life of man and he has brought esthetic values into his life, but in Paradise on Earth, it will be pervasive. The qualities inspired by beautiful things and ideas will be magnified and will extend to everyone.

Man and nature once again will be in perfect balance. Cities will once more become pleasant and comfortable to inhabit, and townscapes will become the epitome of harmony between the man-made and the natural, between the spiritual and material. Artistic and literary masterpieces created in the Age of Night will be treasured in the new world, and our finest artistic heritage will be expanded and developed in abundant, new works of art that will fill everyone's life.

Freedom from Evil

Gradually and naturally, beginning with God's judgment, human souls will be led onward in the path to salvation. Earthly paradise will be virtually free from war and poverty, as well as sickness, and despite the persistence of some clouds at the outset, the soul of everyone there will have been sufficiently purified so that any remaining evil cannot affect it. Simultaneously with the fading of vestigial evil, people will progress in their preparation for the ultimate encounter with the divine.

Everyone will enjoy genuine good health, both physically and spiritually, and will live his life to the full. Health is a wonderful gift, for it allows a person to devote all his power to his mission from God. After a fruitful life, he will die a natural death, happy and content at having fulfilled his God-given mission.

Upon death, the body and spirit separate, for the body can function no longer. But the soul undergoes a period of purification in the spiritual world. We can think of death as freeing the soul to start its journey towards salvation. A soul that is already very saintly is ready upon death for the encounter with the divine, but in the early phase of earthly paradise, few will reach that state. Most will go to the threshold of heaven, where they are led to grow in understanding and love of God before entering the highest level of the spiritual ladder. When earthly paradise has advanced considerably and the human state in general approaches spiritual perfection, all souls will achieve salvation, for they will have grown so much in godliness as to be almost one with the divine.

Measured in our time, however, earthly paradise will not soon develop to that stage of perfection. Before it does, two significant and closely related changes will occur. One is that Johrei will become less and less necessary, until finally only prayers will suffice. The other is that contemplation will come to dominate the mode of existence and the being of everyone, deeply affecting one's inner attitude towards God.

Prayer and Contemplation

To elaborate on the first, Johrei today is a means to cure afflictions that are rooted in the Age of Night. Even after the judgment, it will be necessary to purify the clouds remaining in the spiritual body system, but the divine light will be incomparably stronger than it is now. If people suffer in any way, they will be given relief quickly and easily by Johrei. Furthermore, the fact that people will have ceased to transgress the laws of God means that they will be spiritually much purer to begin with. They will experience no more of the complex, terrible diseases that have begun to ravage our world, and Johrei as a healing method will eventually lose its function altogether.

Prayer will suffice to solve any problem, for prayer is a form of communication with God. In earthly paradise, God's response will be direct and unambiguous, given the great depth of people's love for and understanding of the divine, and the high degree to which their thoughts reflect that understanding.

Now, as in the past, we are given complete freedom in what we think. We may direct all our thoughts to God and to the great expanse of the universe He created, or we may fill our hearts with petty desires, complaints, or evil thoughts. A person can think, wish, or feel in any way he chooses, but his thoughts and feelings at any given time are automatically registered in the spiritual world. Sometimes they cause disturbing upsets and change in the realm of spirit, which, as we have seen, are eventually projected into the realm of matter. Thus, it is in the human heart that wars between nations, conflicts between individuals, and other forms of strife originate.

The freedom of will therefore carries with it moral responsibility for the consequences of all one's thoughts, words, and acts. God is aware of every single movement in our hearts and minds, but during the Age of Night He does not reprimand us right away, even if they are evil. He lets us reap the fruit of the seeds we sow and patiently waits for our repentance. With the advent of the Age of Day, however, people will seek of their own accord to live always in conformity with God's will and to carry out their missions faithfully. They will not struggle with decisions. They may still not be perfect, hence not totally immune to wrongdoing, but God will immediately make clear whether their thoughts and behavior are commendable or reprehensible in His eyes.

As earthly paradise moves into its advanced stages, people's inner attitudes towards God will directly affect more and more aspects of daily life. Those whose souls are closer to God will be so much of the same heart that they can communicate without verbalizing their thoughts and feelings. By this stage, contemplation will have become the mode of existence for everyone. God will have given them such highly refined powers of spiritual perception that they can at last see His will directly and perfectly understand what is in the hearts and minds of others.

In its ultimate phase, Paradise on Earth will be so perfect, so unblemished, that it may be called the Crystal World. All evil and hatred will have been cleansed away. The world will have become the final realization of absolute goodness and love. Completely free from even a hint of sin or impurity, humankind at last will dwell in the heavenly abode longed for through the ages. This is the Crystal World of unity with God.

Part Two
DYNAMICS OF SPIRITUAL HEALING

In Part 2, the focus of discussion shifts from the spiritual and religious implications of Johrei to its practical application. Mr. Okada believed that optimum health, both in body and spirit, is essential if a person is to carry out his God-given mission in this world. No matter how robust a person may appear, he is not truly healthy as long as his spiritual body system is clouded. In this sense, most of us today are in the state of apparent health, or pseudo-health, because of heavy clouds in our bodies. If the clouds in each of us kept on accumulating indefinitely, not only would we lose the vitality necessary to function as normal human beings, but ultimately our species would simply perish, having lost the strength to live. Fortunately, the human body has the innate ability to cleanse its systems and eradicate the clouds through what Mr. Okada called the process of purification. Many familiar symptoms of illness, uncomfortable and painful as they may be, are actually signs of ongoing purification. Not cognizant of the essentially beneficial nature of purification, people have consistently sought to suppress or eliminate such symptoms, thinking them detrimental to their health. Johrei helps to get at the cause by breaking up and dispelling the clouds effectively and with minimum discomfort, thereby contributing to the optimum health of the recipient. It is hoped that medical science will benefit by adding and expanding the spiritual dimension and incorporating the concept of purification and the method of Johrei into its colossal system of knowledge.—Eds.

3

New Frontiers for Medicine

Spiritual Dimension of Health

DIVINE providence is guiding man to build a new world where goodness will be the active, dominant force of life and where the evil of sin and ambivalence of guilt no longer control human behavior or thinking. Earthly paradise will set the stage for man's initial venture into a mode of peace and happiness that will prevail until people are ready for final salvation and eternal life in heaven. Not all of us will know the new world. Those who do not genuinely repent and receive God's forgiveness will not survive the divine judgment, and they will never experience the great joy of building Paradise on Earth and living in full accord with God's will.

Total Well-being

God created us to share in the unfolding of His plan. The sanctity of human life derives solely from that awesome fact. To serve God, every one of us must be aware of his mission and work gladly at it as long as he is able, holding fast to the path set for him. We must pledge all our strength to fulfilling the role God has given each of us to play. Spiritual and physical health is the essential condition that enables us to accomplish our individual missions. Until people become both spiritually and physically whole, true civilization will remain only a hope.

The state of our health today is not good; we are hindered by uneven or bad health. That being so, how can people attain real health, the kind of total well-being I call wholeness? First, we must discard the notion that a human being is an assemblage of distinct parts. The human body is a unified, integrated entity that is both material and spiritual. Some disorder in one part of the body affects not only that particular area but other parts as well. Actually, the fact that the various physical ailments of man are often symptoms of problems that lie elsewhere is becoming more and more widely recognized today. As we are beginning to realize, it is no longer possible to assume that a disease can be cured by treating only symptoms, or localizing treatment to a specific area.

The tendency to compartmentalize disease, to think of it as physical, emotional, or mental, and no more, also is a mistake. I spoke earlier of the spiritual and physical body systems, which are identical in shape and structure and inseparable until death. Although they are perfectly integrated, only the physical body system is visible and palpable. But the spiritual system, although we cannot see or feel it, is equally vulnerable and can be contaminated. Further, the conditions of the spiritual system are reflected in the physical, usually with some time lag. Thus, any psychosomatic, mental, even physiological disorder has a spiritual dimension that we cannot ignore if we are to be cured of an ailment completely and permanently. It is essential that we accept the spiritual and material integration of the human body. And if we do, we can also accept the genuineness of Johrei, a method of healing that treats the health of body and spirit as one and the same.

Contamination of the Body

Impurities in the spiritual body system take the form of clouds, which accumulate partly as projections of the clouds on the soul, but predominantly as the result of human activities that run counter to the spiritual laws governing life and nature. Among those laws, the original purposes of created things and the principle of purification are particularly relevant. When the clouds have accumulated beyond a certain amount, they begin to weaken our will and intellect and undermine our vitality. That makes it harder for us to perform our missions satisfactorily. If clouds were allowed to keep on contaminating our spiritual bodies without relief, we would soon cease to be functional entities. Without some chance for their occasional eradication, the clouds would incapacitate too many people, finally putting the very survival of the human race in jeopardy.

Fortunately, however, the divine principle of purification is at work here. God endowed us with a natural ability to eliminate impurities as the need arises. Although various kinds of physical discomfort usually accompany the spiritual process of purification, it should be understood as a blessing, a God-given function that cleanses our body systems so as to enable us to carry on our missions. Any attempt to deter the purifying function artificially contradicts the divine will and the laws of the spiritual realm.

One inevitably inherits a considerable volume of clouds from one's parents, but even more are newly generated by introducing into the body things that God did not mean for ingestion. These include unpalatable substances foreign to or unnatural for the human organism. By consuming such substances in defiance of the spiritual laws of creation, we cause not only clouds to form in the immaterial body, but certain toxic substances to appear in the physical body. We call the latter "toxins."* It must be noted, however, that unlike toxic substances in the medical sense, they are the material reflections of clouds. They are quite different from conventional toxins.

Self-cleansing Action

Toxins accumulate in parts of the physical body that correspond to the clouded areas of the spiritual body. Any increment of clouds in the spiritual system is accompanied by a proportionate increase of toxins in the

---

* The idea of toxins remains hypothetical insofar as their existence has yet to be scientifically verified, but it helps explain the spiritual process of purification in physical terms. It is possible to interpret toxins both as infinitesimal matter and in terms of abnormalities in the genes, tissues, and bodily functions.—Eds.

physical. When clouds thicken in the spiritual body, toxins follow suit by hardening, and when clouds are dispelled, toxins, too, are eliminated. When purification sets in, the physical body system undergoes an elimination crisis as it tries to excrete toxins. Thus, the process of purification is echoed physically in the dissolution and excretion of toxins.

We should recognize the positive contribution purification makes to better health, for it is one of the greatest blessings God has bestowed upon us. Purification is indeed a blessing, for the presence of clouds hinders people from fulfilling their responsibilities. Only those who are free from spiritual impurities are able to live fully, in perfect health.

Today, virtually everyone has clouds in the spiritual body system and toxins in the physical system. In fact, the systems of many people are so heavily clouded and so contaminated by toxins that they do not have the vitality to benefit sufficiently from their self-cleansing capacity. More often than not, such people appear robust but are not truly healthy; their vitality is so sapped that the process of purification simply remains temporarily suspended or dormant in them.

As the end of the Age of Night approaches to usher in the Age of Day, out of the spiritual world will come ever stronger purificatory power. All of us will be forced to undergo intense purification. It is to prepare for this eventuality that God has given us the power of Johrei to dispel the clouds and eliminate the toxins that have accumulated to excess in our body systems.

CLOUDS AND TOXINS

Since the eradication of clouds in the spiritual body system is essential to genuine health, we must not restrain the purificatory functions of the body. We must understand the process of purification and appreciate its positive contribution to the state of our own body and spirit. To dispel clouds and prevent new ones from forming, we must know that clouds appear in the immaterial body, originating predominantly in acts that violate the spiritual laws of creation. Suppression of purification is itself one such act; it not only blocks the expulsion of clouds, but actually increases their presence in the spiritual body system.

As explained earlier, "purification" refers to the whole process ordained by God of eradicating clouds from the spiritual body system. During the process, an elimination crisis occurs in the physical body, producing various symptoms usually associated with sickness. We tend to interpret them simply as pathological, but more accurately, they are an indication that the body is ridding itself of impurities. We continue to regard those physiological or mental symptoms only negatively, as signs of bad health, when in fact they may signify improving health.

Proscribed Materials

Early in history, man learned to lighten physical suffering by using vegetable, animal, and mineral remedies. Even before the time of Hippocrates, and Shen Nung in

China, who legend says was the first emperor to use herbs in easing the suffering of the sick, people in diverse parts of the world discovered that certain substances really did mitigate, if temporarily, pain and other kinds of discomfort. Soon the belief became widespread that herbal and other medicines could cure disease, but people did not realize that they contain substances not intended for human consumption or application to the body.

Long before God created man, He had already created everything He considered necessary for human life. God endowed the land, the seas, lakes, and rivers with powers that could help sustain life, and to the air, sun, moon and stars, and to the plants and minerals also, He gave each its own set of properties that would be beneficial to man. God also created many different kinds of foods so that each local environment provided enough to sustain human health, and He designated what man can eat and what he cannot. God gave man the ability to taste and gave flavor to foods so that he could distinguish between what is appropriate and what should be avoided.

We are made so that when our bodies are in need of nourishment, we feel hunger or thirst for the kinds of foods that will provide the proper nutritional elements— minerals, vitamins, carbohydrates for energy, protein for tissue building, liquids for body fluids. In exercising the freedom that God gave us, however, increasingly we have distorted the taste, smell, appearance, and nutritional value of foods. When we consume these "treated" foods, we temporarily fool our natural desire. While proper foods can be digested and assimilated, distorted or proscribed materials not only are incompletely digested but cannot be completely eliminated by the body. Consuming proscribed materials, because that, too, is an act against the spiritual laws of life and nature, generates clouds in the immaterial body, which give rise to toxic substances in the physical system. Medicines contain potent substances that cannot be assimilated, and they remain inside to contaminate the body systems.

Modern medical science has developed many refined and sophisticated practices, particularly with regard to the physical repair of accidental and chronic injury. Advances in surgical techniques and the discovery of antibiotics are among its most notable achievements. At the same time, however, it has moved further away from even the central teachings of Hippocrates, who emphasized the healing power of nature assisted by healthful food and environment. The basic ideas of modern medicine arose centuries ago, and over all this time they have been encouraging the use of unassimilable substances as healing agents. Thus, medicine today has become a highly systematized art of alleviating or eliminating physical suffering, but it does not reduce—in fact, it often increases—toxins.

Elimination Crises

As a result, people of our time are rarely free from toxins derived from medicines. We tend to assume that if there are no immediate, violent reactions to a given medication or treatment, it is probably harmless, regardless of whether it "cures" us or not. But the toxins that form in the physical body from those substances remain there for many years. Sooner or later, they must be excreted. If they keep on increasing indefinitely, they will reduce the vitality of the person until he can no longer function normally.

Perhaps most medical scientists today recognize the fundamental validity of natural healing, through food and environment, but few have ever tried to determine the nature of toxins and their role in physical afflictions, much less their relation to clouds in the spiritual body system. Toxins take many different forms and act in any number of ways depending on the individual's genetic inheritance and physical, emotional, and spiritual state. Toxins may circulate in the form of impurities in the blood or lymph fluid, or they may congeal to produce hardened masses in certain areas of the body as it tries to neutralize and store them until the onset of an elimination crisis. Sometimes toxins take the form of extremely rarefied and elusive substances that can move freely and instantaneously from one part of the body to another. When clouds in the spiritual body are eradicated, toxins, too, are dissolved and eliminated from the physical body along with sputum, nasal discharge, perspiration, pus, mucus, bleeding, or some other excreted substance.

A massive presence of toxins contaminates the blood, exerts pressure on the internal organs, erodes the tissue*

---

* It is conjectured that the toxins eventually find their way deep into the nucleus of cells and deform the genes. Presumably, the disruptive influence of toxins extends to the most minute level of matter that constitutes a human cell.—Eds.

in the area where they are concentrated, and lowers the functional vitality of the body. Lower vitality means that a person's eliminative capacity is reduced.* Under those conditions, toxins remain in the tissue, increasing and hardening more with passing time. Still, they cannot just go on accumulating; eventually, toxins will be excreted, but the greater the volume, the more entangled and serious the elimination crisis.

Purification takes place only when impurities are present, spiritually as clouds and materially as toxins. Another necessary condition to get the process going is a self-cleansing power—or vitality—strong enough to start it. However, a number of secondary factors may trigger an elimination crisis. They include environmental factors such as climatic changes, polluted air and water, inferior public hygiene, and excessive sunlight; bacteria and viruses, food poisoning, etc.; injuries and burns; allergies; strain, fatigue from overwork or overexertion, and psychological and spiritual factors. How these secondary factors influence the intensity, location, and symptoms of the elimination crisis is contingent upon the nature, type, amount, location, and age of the toxins that have accumulated.

Incomplete Metabolism

Toxins vary according to the nature of the clouds they reflect, and according to the kinds and amounts of im-

* Generally, young people, the rural population, and the citizens of less developed countries have a relatively greater eliminative capacity than older persons, city dwellers, and people in industrial societies. The latter tend to have more toxins.—Eds.

proper foods, medicines, prepared chemicals, or other foreign substances we ingest. Our physical, emotional, and spiritual states also influence the production and accumulation of toxins. Improper foods or combinations cannot be metabolized completely even by the magnificent body God has given us. And proper foods and combinations themselves may not be completely metabolized if they are consumed when we are under emotional or physical stress. Unnatural, prolonged confinement for patients, lack of regular exercise, unpleasant news, or some activity that disturbs the tranquility of meals, and so on may cause such stress and interfere with proper digestion and metabolism.

In sum, foods incompletely metabolized, for whatever reason, become toxins that the body may not be able to discharge through its regular processes and channels. After storing them for some amount of time, the body acts to eliminate the accumulated toxins in response to one kind of stimulus or another. We then experience the pain and discomfort of the elimination crisis, conditions symptomatic of illness. The medicines and other foreign substances we take to suppress those symptoms add further to the toxic burden on our bodies. Over the years and generations, toxins do substantial damage, in the long run undermining our well-being and thwarting our attempts to carry out our missions.

The type and nature of toxins and our daily mode of behavior at home and at work determine where in the body the toxins will tend to congeal, and therefore, what kind of symptoms will accompany their dissolution and elimination. Toxins that have coagulated behind the heart, for example, are likely to cause malfunction in that vital organ. Similarly, toxins congealed in the back of the stomach are often responsible for gastric disorders. In general, the excretion of toxins derived from Western medicines produces acute pain, while the suffering is less severe but more prolonged when toxins from Chinese medicines are eliminated.

Congenital and Acquired

Toxins can be classified into several categories by their origin or source, but one of the most important distinctions is between congenital and acquired toxins. Congenital toxins,* what one inherits from one's parents, often have been passed on from one generation to another over long periods, even centuries. These toxins are the product of harmful substances that were ingested by one's ancestors. Acquired toxins derive from impure substances entering the body after one's birth. Those substances include various kinds of medications, but another source of acquired toxins is food contaminated by fertilizers, insecticides, and other agricultural chemicals, composts, artificial food additives, and so forth.

We cannot date the first use of fertilizer because the cultivation of plants is ancient beyond record, but we can be certain that fertilized farming is very, very old. Most agricultural societies used fertilizer of some sort long before chemical substances were introduced, but applying foreign matter, organic or chemical, to edible plants

---

* Possibly they are transmitted both in the form of clouds and as genetic information.—Eds.

is contrary to the spiritual laws governing life and nature. Like medicine, fertilizer always leaves impurities behind that keep accumulating, thereby contaminating the soil. In fertilized and chemically sprayed plants, the volume of impurities in the plant decreases somewhat by the time it bears fruit, but they never really disappear, and the soil is deprived of its natural fertility.

It is relatively easy to do away with fertilizer, for what I call nature farming* will yield pure, natural produce without any fertilizer or agricultural chemicals. Far more difficult is to discontinue the use of medicine, for it has played such a large role in man's history, as I shall discuss later. But here again, Johrei comes as a ray of hope for people today, the majority of whom are overburdened with impurities in their body systems. It offers them a way to begin changing their life-styles and reconsider some of the assumptions behind established concepts of health. Ultimately, however, we cannot cleanse ourselves of clouds without the help of faith in God, and no path but genuine repentance will lead to perfect health and true happiness.

Physical Effects of Purification

Let me now explain the process of purification in terms of how it manifests itself in the realm of matter. Basically purification is a spiritual phenomenon

---

* The Japanese term *shizen nōhō* could be rendered as "natural farming," but in order to distinguish it from organic agriculture, we have translated it as "*nature* farming."—Eds.

involving the eradication of clouds, but it is always accompanied by an action of eliminating toxins from the physical body system. Just as clouds are reflected materially as toxins, the process of purification is echoed in the physical system by an elimination crisis.

Elementary Purification

Toxins accumulate in different parts of the body, and they coagulate over time until the process of purification begins. As long as toxins remain in hardened form, they obstruct blood circulation and the normal functioning of body organs nearby. Stiff neck and shoulders, heaviness of the head, blurred vision, impaired hearing and sense of smell, malfunctioning of the heart, liver, kidneys, and so forth, all indicate the presence of coagulated toxins in the areas concerned. These conditions tear down the will and ability to work and prevent a person from fully performing his or her mission as a human being.

Most of us today have so many toxins in our bodies that occasional mild purification is essential in order to stay in reasonably good health. Despite the temporary misery it brings us, without this self-cleansing action, we would gradually become so saturated with clouds and toxins that the strength to live would wane, until one by one we all perished.

Many of the discomforts that characterize an elimination crisis are familiar, but few people are aware of what they signify—that the blood is being cleansed as toxins are dissolved and purged from the body. Fever has an especially vital function in the excretion of coagulated toxins. Purificatory energy emanating from the realm of spirit is necessary to eradicate clouds in the spiritual body system. Materially, it takes the form of heat that dissolves toxins, which is precisely what fever is.

In a typical case of mild purification, some of the dissolved toxins immediately enter the lungs. If they are watery and thin, these toxins can be eliminated relatively easily, mixed with phlegm and sometimes with night-sweat or urine. If they are thick, they remain there for a time and are excreted primarily through the trachea by the pumping action of coughing, and secondarily through nasal discharge or diarrhea. A headache, sore throat, otitis media, inflammation of the lymph glands, and aching joints, or pain in the inguinal lymph glands are all features of an elimination crisis commonly observed during the elementary stage of purification.

If we think of these symptoms as signs of the natural and rational self-cleansing action of the body, we are able to accept them as something quite different from the unsolicited misfortune that they usually appear to be. If a person lets nature have its way without trying to suppress the symptoms, elementary purification will run its course unobstructed and he will recover. His health will be better than ever, particularly if a large volume of toxins has been purged from his body. To undergo the process of purification at this level prevents a more severe elimination crisis from occurring later.

Danger of Suppression

Nonetheless, most of us do everything possible to suppress the symptoms of an elimination crisis without realizing that they are signs of purification. Afraid even of a fever, we try to reduce any temperature above "normal." Artificial depression of fever suspends the dissolution of toxins and encourages their recoagulation, upon which coughing and other symptoms of the elimination crisis recede, but any semblance of recovery is too often only superficial and temporary. Although the symptoms seem to disappear, and the person has apparently gotten well, such suppressive methods are tying the hands trying to help. Purification is thwarted—but not altogether. It is suspended, only to recur later in a renewed attempt by the body to excrete an even greater amount of toxins. The containment of elimination crises by suppressive methods often protracts, even aggravates, the condition, or sometimes it leads to recurrence, accompanied by more virulent, more complicated symptoms.

Most medicines contain substances our bodies cannot assimilate, substances God did not mean for us. But almost everyone uses them, believing that they are the most effective way to relieve pain and discomfort. Actually, they do the job very well by reducing fever and killing the bacteria that help prod the dissolution and excretion of toxins, but they are not designed to eliminate toxins, or their spiritual form, clouds. Instead, medicines and drugs block the purification process without getting at the real source of suffering.

Every time the cleansing action is suppressed by artificial means, the old toxins recoagulate and new ones accumulate until secondary purification is necessary. When a person is filled with vitality, drastic purification will occur, as though nature were suddenly demanding full repayment of accumulated debts. A fever high enough to dissolve the large volume of toxins develops, phlegm increases, coughing becomes more intense, and breathing is difficult. Drastic purification, too, should be left to proceed with the aid only of Johrei, for the patient will recover quite naturally when enough toxins have been excreted in some form or other. But, using all manner of treatments, we interrupt the purification process, and each time we do, while symptoms may temporarily be alleviated, it gets harder to suppress because the toxins grow more abundant. Increasingly stronger drugs that work more quickly and efficiently are given as the condition worsens; milder drugs can no longer effectively control the severe pains and discomfort of the elimination crises occurring with drastic purification.

Escalator Syndrome

Another kind of secondary purification takes place in a body system with limited cleansing capacity—slow purification. As in the case of drastic purification, an infection is usually what starts the process going, but only in the presence of toxins. Disease germs cannot live or multiply without toxins, which begin to liquefy and enter the lungs at the onset of the elementary purification process. If purification is left to proceed unimpeded until the toxic substance is eliminated, the body will return to normal. In administering artificial treatments, however, we block the purge of liquefied toxins—some of which combine with viscid mucus secreted internally to produce phlegm—from the lungs. Excretion of phlegm being blocked, toxins are trapped in the lungs, where they gradually harden again. It is important to allow toxins to be excreted, lest bacteria in the affected area multiply until they damage the tissue.

Once a patient reaches the stage where he has a slight but constant fever, he is often given one or more kinds of drugs. Even taken in small amounts they protract the condition, but the usual tendency is to take them in ever-increasing doses. Such treatments enervate the patient. Even a robust body would be weakened under them, and they reduce its self-cleansing capacity considerably. The symptoms fade until there is no fever, no coughing, and no phlegm is discharged. Everyone is pleased, believing that recovery is in sight. What happens is that the body regresses to its prepurification state. Worse, the patient has by then accumulated more toxins and his physical vitality has been drained further. His problem may become temporarily dormant, but that is a far cry from healing. With some kind of stimulation, the coagulated toxins begin to dissolve again and move towards an outlet, upon which his symptoms may suddenly reemerge. Or, worse, the patient will suffer from a more complex syndrome than before.

Both drastic and slow purification are common phenomena among people everywhere, and they will continue to occur as long as we persist in suppressing the symptoms of elementary purification by artificial treatments. In the same way, suppressing secondary purification, whether slow or drastic, with superpotent drugs has given rise to many new, dreaded diseases, which in no way can be seen as the blessing that purification really is.

Medical treatment reduces fever and alleviates pain and other symptoms, but it also works to postpone purification. A permanent cure requires the eradication of clouds/toxins; it can be achieved only by cleansing the body to eliminate the conditions that make it vulnerable. Johrei transmits purificatory power to eradicate clouds in the spiritual body, thereby dissolving toxins and helping the body to eject more of them without any severe pain or discomfort.

AN INTEGRATED SCIENCE OF MEDICINE

The remarkable achievements in recent years in every branch of science, including medicine and pharmacology, have made it possible to gain an increasingly deeper understanding of the disease process. Indeed, the unfolding of God's providence itself is partly revealed in the progress of science.

Perceptions of Disease

Current and expected advances in medical science and technology increase the range of tools with which practitioners can study the disease process. If properly applied, the knowledge gained could materially aid the practitioner in managing the purification process effectively according to the nature of the toxins, the strength of the patient, and related factors. Essential to such a development is a new perception of disease. We must stop thinking of the condition of illness as an enemy attacking innocent people, and begin to see in it the benefits of a purification process that occurs because there is a long-standing accumulation of toxins in the body. It is imperative that the skills, patience, and understanding of physicians be channeled into teaching us how to live so as to prevent toxins from accumulating, and how best to help our bodies eliminate those we have acquired or inherited.

Medical scientists have done much over the centuries to develop methods to relieve the various symptoms of an unhealthy condition. Antibiotics and highly refined surgical techniques, in particular, have been applied in a great many cases of diseases once considered incurable and have frequently saved the victims from imminent death. Preventive medicine, also, has been instrumental in combating epidemics. Unfortunately, however, successes in the alleviation of the *symptoms* of disease continue to let the profession ignore the spiritual dimension of disease, especially the beneficial aspect of purification. Indeed, the assumptions that guide the practice of medicine need to be reexamined and broadened.

First of all, it is important that medical people begin to understand that suppressing the purification process is dangerous, and becoming more so. It not only blocks the purging of toxins, but actually increases their presence inside the body. Toxins whose excretion has been frustrated by herbs, drugs, surgery,* acupuncture,** or other suppressive measures may, when the body finally attempts to get rid of them, cause more serious elimination crises years after they were suppressed. Similarly, vaccines designed to induce immunity inhibit the purification process. These preventive medical agents, even a small amount, may effectively contain the toxins and immunize a person against a particular infectious disease. But in the long run, they artificially deter purification and often cause severe elimination crises later and in future generations.

Again, modern medical theory holds bacteria and viruses directly responsible for infectious disease—and they do play a crucial role in initiating an elimination crisis. Vaccines and drugs, however, kill these microorganisms or render them inactive, thereby weakening the eliminative capacity of the body and suppressing the purification process. If toxins kept on building up with repeated suppression, eventually the accumulated volume would jeopardize that person's life and even affect the health of his descendants for several generations. Without some way to break out of this vicious circle, humankind would sooner or later die out.

---

* Surgical removal of the tonsils, for example, often obstructs the elimination of toxins that have accumulated in the upper part of the body. Similarly, it is not advisable to remove the appendix, for that organ plays an important role in the excretion of toxins from the lower part of the body.
** This ancient cure helps to relieve pain temporarily by hardening a mass of toxins in the part of the body punctured with needles.

Apparent Health

Medical science has developed many ways of effectively suppressing purification, often with minimal use of medications. New drugs, moreover, appear all the time, each one more efficient than the last in its palliative effects and yet considerably slower in causing an elimination crisis. The sophistication of medicine certainly has helped to prolong the average lifespan,* especially in the populations of advanced societies. Those people not only have greater access to medical treatment, but also eat more fertilized and artificially processed foods, etc. Actually, they live longer precisely because of, rather than in spite of, the drain on vitality that occurs as more toxins accumulate and harden.

More people than ever appear to lead healthy and active lives even in their old age, but no drug has lifted the threat of illness. Just as soon as "old" diseases seem to have been driven out of the picture, "new," increasingly complex ailments appear. This is a consequence of our having concentrated on suppressing symptoms of the purification process. Virtually everyone today has a large amount of toxins in his body. An appearance of good health is possible because the presence of excessive toxins lowers a person's vitality so drastically, or potent modern drugs solidify the toxins so

---

* Another important factor in increased longevity is the significantly reduced infant mortality rate, which is due in large part to improved sanitation and higher standards of living. It should also be remembered that war and hunger, as well as sickness, are major statistical components of the mortality rate.—Eds.

effectively, that purging action cannot take place as easily as it should.

To describe the state where toxins are present but purifying action is dormant or has not yet produced an elimination crisis, we use the term "pseudo-health," for the person *appears* to be perfectly healthy. The case when illness does not occur because the body is free of clouds and toxins is extremely rare, but that is the only instance of true health. Actually, probably no one has true health, which is unfortunate, because if we were free from clouds and toxins, we could live in good health to one hundred twenty years. But most people die from disease long before their allotted time. Few live out their life to the full.

Since we all have clouds and toxins in our bodies, we live in a state of pseudo-health and always have some symptom, dormant or active. It may be only a headache or stiff neck for some, while for others it may be shortness of breath or fever at even the slightest exertion. Some people are susceptible to colds, others are hypersensitive to certain foods and suffer from abdominal pains or diarrhea. It is not surprising that many people have no confidence in their own bodies and are plagued by uneasiness. The action of purification can happen anytime in even apparently healthy people, often without warning, and this ever-present possibility creates the anxiety of not knowing what to expect.

True Rationality

Until now, during the Age of Night, the purificatory

power emanating from the realm of spirit has been relatively weak. That is one reason why medical methods of suppressing purification have worked remarkably well, despite all their negative implications for the long run. Since we entered the period of transition to the Age of Day, however, the spiritual world has been sending forth ever stronger purificatory energy. This is going to mean, on the one hand, the growing intensity and frequency of elimination crises and the necessity of more and more superpotent drugs to deal with them. On the other hand, Johrei as a method of transmitting purificatory power to the spiritual body of a patient will gain in effectiveness with the passage of time.

From now on, suppressive methods of treatment will become less feasible as the Age of Day approaches and the spiritual world grows brighter. People will find it exceedingly difficult to maintain even a semblance of strong health, for all will be forced to undergo unprecedentedly severe elimination crises. Extremely powerful drugs and treatments will be the only way to contain a purification process of such intensity, and even the most advanced therapies may not work; if they are effective, it will be only at the risk of the patient's life. Worse still, continued attempts at artificial suppression will create a serious threat to health, bringing the widespread misery of terminal or incurable diseases of one kind or another. Like it or not, we will have to give up all suppressive therapies before it is too late and rely only on such methods as will truly contribute to genuine health.

Man has devised a variety of ways to combat disease, beginning with the magico-religious healing methods of our primitive forbears. Modern medical science represents the culmination of rationalistic medicine that originated in the ancient world; it stands at the apex of the colossal system of knowledge man has built up about his biological existence.

Scientific medicine, in fact, has overshadowed the long and rich traditions of spiritual medicine that were once seen everywhere. They have been driven to the remote corners of civilization. Many types of faith healing have been relegated to the realm of superstition. In most cases it was right to discredit them, but in no way does that mean spiritualism in medicine will be, or should be, completely destroyed by rationalism. Sooner or later medical science must recognize its own deficiency and augment its practice and system of knowledge with the spiritual dimension.

Medicine will be elevated to a higher plane of truth and rationality when the scientific and spiritual approaches are integrated. Johrei and the concept of purification underlying it constitute such an integrated approach. Johrei is not an alternative medicine, but it makes medical science complete, filling the gaps in the foundations of rationalistic medicine. When medical science incorporates purification into its conceptual system and Johrei into its methodology, it will become a true science of healing that seeks to make pseudo-health into true health by clearing away all clouds and toxic impurities.

4

The Way of Nature

Transmission of Johrei

Of all creation, man alone is given the special task of fulfilling God's will for this world, and because human existence is governed directly and totally by divine power, man cannot even begin that task without His merciful help. It is God's wish that we live a genuinely good life, and be healthy and free from suffering so that we may carry out His plan. Yet the problem of health, happiness, and fulfillment cannot be resolved by human ability alone. We must approach life and the problem of health from a perspective that embraces more than just the physical, for our well-being depends on our spiritual condition as well as our physiological or mental state.

Two Alternatives

We have already discussed how clouds form in the spiritual body system as a result of acts that run counter to the laws of creation, and we have shown how they are reproduced in material form as toxins in the physical body system. When enough impurities have gathered, the purification process sets in to disperse the clouds, thereby causing an elimination crisis in the physical body.

If clouds are responsible for our afflictions, we must do everything we can to dispel them from our bodies, and we must finally eliminate their sources. We noted that people inherit impurities from their parents. There are external sources of clouds and toxins, also, which range from unpalatable plants and fertilized foods to drugs and chemicals. Ideally, we should stop ingesting any substance that God did not create for human consumption, but that is actually quite difficult. The constant intrusion of many such substances is built into modern life-styles, whether we like it or not. Moreover, even if we could avoid the external sources of impurities altogether, we would still be burdened with the clouds and toxins that have accumulated in our bodies since birth, on top of what we have inherited from many generations past.

What should and can we do to cleanse our bodies? Letting purification take its natural course of action is one way. Understanding the intrinsic value of purification to human health and letting it proceed smoothly is the first step in gaining freedom from impurities. Given the large amounts of spiritual and material impurities most of us now carry, however, it would take years of constant purification to eliminate even a substantial portion of them. It is probably impossible to cleanse the body completely in a lifetime. In the meantime, people

continue to suffer one illness after another, which undermines their efforts to do what God intended for them in
this world. Some conditions grow so severe as to keep
people in bed for years, others turn out to be fatal. Simply
to leave purification unimpeded is, therefore, actually
impractical. In any case, this alternative does not guarantee that one will attain true health.

Another alternative is religious. A person of deep faith
who leads a life of constant prayer and dedication to God
will be able, by grace, to eradicate the clouds on his soul,
and impurities in his spiritual body system will also decrease. But no matter how pure his soul, as long as he
retains substantial amounts of clouds and toxins in his
body systems, he will inevitably undergo purification
from time to time. If his pain and discomfort are un-
bearable, he will perhaps turn to some therapy that is
likely to cause more impurities to accumulate in his
body. A more practical problem with this alternative is
how many of us, in this day and age, can long endure an
ascetic life cut off from all influences and temptations that
might lead to evil.

Divine Light

Although each is meaningful in its own way, both
those alternatives are ultimately infeasible, at least for
most people. This is precisely where Johrei has a crucial
role, for it offers a third, and preferable way. As I explained earlier, it is a divine gift given to man in this
time of transition from the Age of Night to the Age of
Day, when the purificatory power of the spiritual world

grows steadily stronger. Johrei effectively combines the other two alternatives, for it is at once a vehicle of spiritual awakening and a method of healing that anyone can practice. Johrei is, moreover, compatible with the basic goals of medicine; it opens up a whole new horizon for medical science by adding the spiritual dimension.

Simply put, Johrei is a method of transmitting divine light to a human body through the palm of its administrator. Divine light here means the purificatory energy emanating from the realm of spirit that cleanses clouds in the spiritual body system. In accordance with the principle of spiritual dominance over the material, once

Giving and receiving Johrei together

clouds in a given area are dispelled, the toxins existing in the same area of the physical body will also be eliminated. With both clouds and toxins gone, the bacteria or viruses that were active in that part of the body are deprived of their habitat and rendered harmless. They, too, are discharged eventually. In this way, Johrei insures that the purification process will be completed smoothly and speedily without much suffering.

When you administer Johrei, you and the recipient should first offer prayers to God. Then, seating the patient opposite you, face to face, raise your hand, with the palm out, towards him. You may use both hands alternately, but never at the same time. There is no need to touch the body of the patient. Hold your hand about a foot away from the area concerned. Your hand and arm should be completely relaxed, since you are transmitting *divine light*, not your own power. You are nothing more than a channel for divine light, and so you must leave everything to God. Except for a sincere wish for the well-being of the recipient, you need not try to muster any extra sentiments or other motives. Simply try to feel the divine light penetrating far into the patient's body. The general rule is to channel Johrei first to the forehead of the receiver. When you are through with the frontal part, have the person turn around so you can transmit from the back. If the patient is unable to move or cannot sit for some reason, you may adapt this rule flexibly. If no one else is available, you may channel Johrei to yourself.

Each session of administering Johrei usually lasts from ten to thirty minutes. In the case of a seriously ill or injured patient, however, try to continue as long as necessary, at intervals of ten to thirty minutes. When each session is over, be certain to give a prayer of thanks to God.

Below are several points that will be useful to remember in administering Johrei. More important than technical details, however, is the attitude of the transmitter. As long as his intent and behavior are honest, expressing the depth of faith he really feels, Johrei given by him will be effective. Preoccupation with technique, on the other hand, is tantamount to ignoring God and His power. Needless to say, Johrei works only when it is practiced for good purposes. One will administer it in vain to achieve an evil or selfish objective.

Feverish Areas

In a nutshell, Johrei should be channeled towards areas where the spiritual body is particularly clouded and where purification is taking place. It is not easy to determine those places exactly, but with experience one can discern certain indications of ongoing purification. The easiest to identify is an external wound. Simply direct Johrei towards the affected area itself. In the case of a headache, it is best to give Johrei primarily to the front and back of the head, and then move to the areas around the neck.

Generally, areas where hardened toxins are dissolving are feverish. Focusing Johrei on those areas is the most effective. In the case of a cold, more often than not fever arises around the neck and shoulders. Coughing and phlegm usually follow inflammation of those regions, which is caused by extra heat generated to dissolve toxins.

Stiffness and swellings often indicate toxic congestion in the area. Brain diseases are usually accompanied by hardened masses of toxins in the area to the left or right of the neck or around the base of the skull. Johrei should be channeled directly to those parts.

In many afflictions it is more effective to concentrate on the back—as opposed to the front—of a person's body in administering Johrei. This is generally true for eye diseases, cardiac and gastric disorders, and kidney ailments. In the case of a stomach disease, you will usually find a feverish area between one of the shoulder blades and the spine. Johrei should be directed to that area.

In directing the divine light of Johrei, among all parts of the body the most careful attention should be given to the head (the crown, front and back), areas around the neck and shoulders, and the back of the kidney region. These are where toxins tend to congeal and, therefore, where elementary purification most often takes place.

Although flexibility is an important feature of Johrei administration, practitioners should observe as suitable a manner as possible. Both the administrator and recipient should be respectful towards each other and express their gratitude before and after the session. Except for an emergency, when one cannot choose the place, a session should be conducted in an appropriately solemn environment.

I would like to mention the seal that believers carry with them. Originally, while praying to God for His help and forgiveness, for each person I wrote the character for "light" on a piece of paper and gave it to him or her. The seal is an expression of an intercessory prayer for the well-being of those who receive Johrei, and a source of spiritual support. Wearing one has proven to give the administrator more confidence, providing him with a tangible symbol of his faith. It serves the bearer as a kind of reminder that he is not alone in his prayers to God. Nonetheless, it is not absolutely necessary for the truly faithful to carry the seal with them, because with or without it, as long as his faith is genuine and his prayer sincere, anyone can administer Johrei.

THE NUTRITION MYTH

We have defined true health as a spiritual and physical state characterized by the total absence of clouds and toxins in the body systems. A person is genuinely healthy when he is pure in spirit and body. He is filled with vitality or self-cleansing capacity, yet without any impurities inside, he does not have to undergo purification. His body is not adversely affected by disease germs or any of the other secondary factors that might otherwise trigger an elimination crisis.

Food and Non-food
By definition, true health is a state virtually no one

can reach in the Age of Night, and in any case, it is not man's goal nor his raison d'être. It is a means to serve an end; true health enables a person to fulfill the mission God gave him in this world, thereby helping him on the long road to the salvation of his soul. Only those who are chosen to participate in earthly paradise will become truly healthy, spiritually and physically whole, and able to live in accordance with the divine will. But we can do something ourselves, starting right now, for the effort to regain better health is in itself an effort to follow God's will, however imperfectly, and God recognizes that fact.

Man is the sum total of what he thinks, what he does, and what he ingests. To the extent that one conforms with the laws of creation in all these things, his spiritual and physical health improves. Conversely, the more one deviates from those laws, the more clouded his spiritual body system becomes. Consciously or unconsciously we continue to act against the spiritual laws of life and nature by ingesting proscribed substances. They cannot be handled by our internal organs, and, ominously, each time more are consumed, more clouds are formed in the spiritual system.

All the great religions, each with its own set of precepts or commandments, warn against wrongdoing. Some also have dietary laws prohibiting certain kinds of food and drink, and they perpetuate dietary taboos, but these are often based on religious or historical circumstances rather than their proven effects on health. Not having any clear criteria on which to base rules against the ingestion of non-food, religions have been unable to counter effectively the misconceptions of modern dietetics and nutrition and the distorted eating habits of the world's people.

There are basically two criteria by which we can differentiate between food and non-food. One is God's intention for the substance in question, and the other is the role He assigned to it. For each of His creatures, God has a clear purpose and assigned a distinct role. When He created the world He gave each region a particular variety of vegetation and wildlife that suited the climate and geological and ecological conditions.* God designated many of those plants and animals as suitable for human consumption, and He gave man the intelligence to invent tools for fishing, hunting, gathering, cultivation, and cooking.

Man's betrayal of God was a crucial turning point in his history. It marked the beginning of his persistent failure from then onwards to observe the spiritual laws of creation. He soon developed the habit of consuming substances originally not meant for human beings. Herbal and mineral medicinal potions are one prime example. As civilization moved ahead, man deviated ever further from the spiritual laws of nature and became more complacently oblivious to the benefits of purification and the harm in forbidden substances. Consequently, people of our time have absorbed all kinds of chemicals, medications, artificial nutrients, synthetic foods, and other improper substances.

* For Mr. Okada, evolution itself is part of God's plan.—Eds.

Natural Diet

Basically, we should eat only those things God intended for us. The human body is made in such a way that it is capable of fully digesting and assimilating any proper foodstuff. No matter what one eats, as long as it is genuine food, the body can process the substance to produce the nourishment necessary to sustain itself. It is best to let the digestive system work as it is meant to; the harder it works, the better it functions to convert food into all the elements required for good health.

A diet that supplies certain nutrients—sometimes in highly concentrated form—that the body is equipped to make itself is unnatural and harmful. Because they are already processed, these specially prepared artificial nutrients and concentrated foods are absorbed almost immediately. When one eats them all the time, the natural body functions tend to degenerate until they become defunct.

In the long run, it is best to eat what one feels like according to one's natural inclinations, without trying to follow some prescribed dietetic pattern. The distortions that have been made in many, if not most, of our foods by additives and preservatives often betray our natural inclinations, however. Many elements needed by the body are missing or out of balance. These distorted foods lack the balance of ingredients needed for proper metabolism, and they can directly cause toxins to arise in the body. Their flavor and stimulant effects mask the true needs of the body. Thus, we need to examine our eating patterns and general condition in some detail to determine whether those natural inclinations have become distorted.

Generally, people who lead an active life find they need about equal proportions of primarily green vegetables and meat. Sick people and the aged need seventy to eighty percent vegetable foods and the remainder animal. The best way to maintain good health is to follow a natural diet, taking no artificial or medicinal substances. Fresh vegetables, raw and green in particular, are an important source of vitality and strength.

Even if a person follows a perfectly natural diet and stops taking all medicines or vitamin pills, he will still not be able to prevent foreign substances from coming into his body system as long as the grains, vegetables, meat, poultry, and fish he consumes are not pure. They are often contaminated by fertilizer, pesticides, and other agricultural chemicals, synthetic additives and preservatives, or polluted soil, air, and water. But there is a way to begin, and that is what I call nature farming.

NATURE FARMING

Just as the human body system has natural nutrient-yielding functions, the soil is endowed with the capacity to produce edible plants sufficient to maintain human life. We might call this inherent ability of the soil "natural power." It is a complex of known properties such as light, heat, water, nitrogen, and bacteria, and also some unknown matter and spiritual elements.

Soil's Power

Nature farming is a method of cultivation designed to let the soil fully exercise its natural power. The basic principle behind the method is quite simple: if a given species of plant is grown on uncontaminated land, the soil will gradually develop the qualities necessary for that particular species. Like human bodies free of clouds and toxins, soil free of unnatural matter is filled with vitality that fully nourishes the plant.

To contaminate the soil with incongruent matter violates the spiritual laws governing creation. Soil mixed with fertilizer, even manure or compost, is robbed of its natural power over a period of time.* Plants, as well, if they are nourished on fertilizer, begin to lose their innate ability to absorb the natural power of the soil. They eventually become totally dependent on fertilizer for survival and growth. How reminiscent that is of modern people; they take so many vitamins and other dietary supplements that the natural digestive and nutrient-yielding functions of their systems slow down until they are defunct.

As plants become dependent on fertilizer and other agricultural chemicals, the more of these substances they absorb, the further they weaken and the greater their

---

* Mr. Okada said that it is permissible to mix chopped rice straw into the soil of paddy fields in cold regions to keep it warm, and to spread cut grass over or in the soil of vegetable fields in special cases to prevent the soil from drying up or hardening. Straw or grass should not be used as organic fertilizer but only as a means to help the soil retain its natural fertility.—Eds.

vulnerability to wind, storm, and blight. Blight is actually a form of purification that occurs as plants and soil cleanse themselves of unnatural matter contained in fertilizer, but if plants are so weakened that they are beyond help, blight will kill them instead of helping them to regain strength. To compound an already bad situation, increasingly more sophisticated insecticides are appearing all the time. They simply generate new impurities that are more damaging than the original ones.

Grains, vegetables, fruit, and other edible plants cultivated by nature farming methods exhibit high resistance to wind, storm and blight. For one thing, their leaves are typically healthier and shorter than those on fertilized plants, and their roots are more vigorous and longer, reaching down deeper into the ground. The fruit itself is usually denser and tastes better than that of fertilized crops. Persons who are seriously ill and cannot eat anything else often find products of nature farming palatable, even delicious, and invariably invigorating.

A Small Step

Nature farming can yield stable crops of better quality than any of the conventional methods of cultivation practiced today. During the first several years after conversion to nature farming, however, the soil in paddy or dry fields continues to be affected by residual impurities that hamper the restoration of its natural power. As a result, the land may not yield good crops for some time, until the soil recovers its original functions.

Another problem that confronts pioneers in nature farming is the scarcity of pure, uncontaminated seeds or bulbs, which come only from pure plants. As in the case of fertilized soil, it takes several generations of seeds and bulbs before their toxic qualities have been cleansed sufficiently. A practitioner of nature farming must have courage and patience to tide him over the initial few years, when his crops may not be as good in quality and quantity as he had hoped. But the long-range results will more than reward his efforts.

Fertilized plants are one of the main routes through which toxic substances invade the human body. Thus, when fertilizer or agricultural chemicals are used, the produce becomes impure, having absorbed things God never intended for it. Ingesting them is an act against the laws of creation, hence it generates clouds in the spiritual body system.

It should be stressed that a proper diet that includes as many products of nature farming as possible is but one small step towards genuine health. Clouds will not diminish, much less disappear, as long as we continue to ingest drugs, medicines, chemicals, or artificially prepared substances. In the long run, because clouds are spiritual impurities, they can be eradicated only through purification or by spiritual means—Johrei, prayers, and repentance.

The principles behind nature farming are analogous to those of purification and Johrei, in that both represent the way of nature, and both essentially concern the spiritual core of what appear to us to be physical phenomena. Johrei healing and nature farming are the antithesis to the overly materialistic thinking that has influenced modern medical and agricultural sciences. Of course, truth is neither exclusively spiritual nor is it only material; it is a synthesis of the two. Just as the medical science of the future must learn how to fully exploit the purificatory power innate to man if it is to advance out of its present state, the agriculture of tomorrow has to find ways to flourish by using the natural power of the soil. If it does not, human health will remain in dire jeopardy. Only a successful effort on both fronts will bring medicine and agriculture to the level of true science that works *for* man, not against him.

Many other fields of human endeavor require wholesale reconsideration in this period of transition from the Age of Night to the Age of Day. As the purificatory energy emanating from the spiritual world grows stronger, the limits of human cognition and perception become increasingly apparent. The very premises of the social sciences, the arts, and education will all have to be fundamentally revised in recognition of the spiritual laws of the universe. Medical science and agriculture are the two areas that need rethinking first, because both bear directly on the health and well-being of man.

Human civilization, if it is to survive God's judgment soon to come, must rise to a higher plane of spirituality where divine law reigns supreme. Johrei and nature farming are but two examples of how man can integrate his religious wisdom and scientific knowledge, and achieve a balanced fusion of his spiritual and material cultures. When man has successfully transformed his civilization along the lines of these ideals, finally he will have built a world of love, peace, and good in Paradise on Earth. Man is, indeed, responsible for his own destiny.

Part Three
PRAYERS AND HYMNS

PRAYER was central in Mr. Okada's daily life, and he was in constant communion with God. He taught that offering prayers to God helps to purify the soul and deepen one's faith. Earnest prayer for others not only brings them peace and happiness, but spiritually elevates the supplicant. To express genuine, deep gratitude to God is a way to demonstrate and develop our love for Him. By glorifying our Lord the Creator, we can partake of the divine kingdom here on earth. Especially during the last years of his ministry, Mr. Okada urged his congregations, "Pray, and you shall commune with the Lord; ask, and you shall receive His grace." Mr. Okada also believed that each word of prayer, whether vocalized or given silently, carries a spiritual force that affects one's inner self and his immediate environment. Prayer, he said, is a potent mystery of faith. A gifted poet, Mr. Okada wrote more than four thousand 31-syllable verses in his lifetime. The earliest ones date back to 1934 when, in preparation for the founding of his own church, he laid down the procedures for morning and evening services. Many of these verses have been combined in thematic groups for use as hymns or prayers. All but one of the prayers presented below in translation are typical of such combined verses. The only exception is the "Prayer of Johrei," which was composed much later by one of his disciples to express the faith, although all the key phrases used therein derive from Mr. Okada's poems and other writings.—Eds.

Prayer of Johrei

GOD of boundless love,
reverently we offer our prayer.
To our teacher you revealed
that the time of judgment is near.
In repentance, we remember our sinful acts
and ask your forgiveness.

You have made known your will
for us, to build on earth your paradise,
free from sickness, poverty, and strife.
You revealed to our teacher your command:
that we are to build a world of perfect
truth, goodness, and beauty,
where your will reigns supreme.

In your forgiveness you gave us your grace
through the divine light of Johrei
to heal the sick and save their lives.
Through the gift of Johrei
you revealed to our teacher
the path of righteousness for humankind.

For our betrayal of your love for us,
for the untold sins
we and our forebears have committed
through all the ages,

we have penitent and humble hearts
in acknowledging our wrongdoing.

God of infinite mercy,
we beg your forgiveness of our sins
and pray that our souls may be purified.
May we, by your grace,
be blessed with purity and strength
to fulfill our mission.
May we build earthly paradise,
and under your protection
achieve ultimate union with you.

O God, Lord of the universe,
hear our prayer
for your blessings and protection.
And if it pleases you,
grant peace and happiness to our souls.

Thanksgiving

O God, Lord of absolute mercy,
we kneel in thanks for your love.
Accept our gratitude for bringing us
   out of ignorance, and
for your patience with our willful ways.

In despair we cursed the world.
We blamed others for our misery.
But your light led us out of suffering
and rescued us from death.

You taught us to love and understand
   each other.
You gave us the power of Johrei
   to heal our distress.
Your abundant blessings on us,
unhappy sinners, never cease.

O God, we, but grains of sand on the shore,
give you our boundless thanks.
We offer ourselves, soul and flesh,
for the fulfillment of your plan.

Give us your grace and guide us
   in our mission, so that
the whole world may know of your love.

In Praise of God

O merciful God, whose greatness is unbounded,
we praise the wonder of your works.
The rainbow flowers adorning meadow and hill,
tall trees with roots deep in the earth,
birds filling the air with merry song and flutter,
and stars that stream through the heavens.

We praise the wonder of your works.

Coming into this world, we suffer from our sins,
but your great mercy helps us on our journey.
You support us as we pass through this world
and you bring us solace from pain.
Our hearts are at peace, filled with joy
in the divine gift of Johrei.

Ceaselessly we praise your love.

Our strength is yours, your staff is our companion.
Your great mercy helps us on our journey.
Your presence dispels our fears,
and you lighten the darkness before us.
The world is lit by your heavenly light;
your love is deep, embracing all without end.

We praise the wonder of your works.

Divine Love

God, Lord of supreme goodness,
to whom our devotion is given.
We cannot measure your love or wisdom
  in their infinity.

You alone are master of the final moment,
you alone know how our final day will dawn.
All the world and our salvation are
  in your hand.

We lift our eyes towards the sky
in contemplation of your infallible wisdom.
We turn our hearts towards heaven, awed
  by your infinite love.

We may be diverted by deception or ignorance,
by splendor that does not serve you.
But gently with justice, you give us
  your love,
as parents do their child.

You always hear a petition that is just.
We pray for your guidance, our hearts open
to the power of Johrei that strengthens
  our faith,
as we seek oneness with you.

Repentance

O God, Supreme Lord of heaven,
once we knew nothing of your saving grace,
trusting only in what we could see and touch.
We were obsessed with self-interest and greed.
We were on the verge of collapse.

Wandering in darkness
with no torch or staff to guide us,
we erected a tower of inferno in our hearts.
Captivated by evil spirits, shamelessly
we continued to fight amongst ourselves.

Blind to God's path right before our eyes,
we marched on down the road
to the hell of doubt and unbelief.
Never reflecting on our own sins,
we blamed others for our plight.

Then we saw a torch in the darkness,
and we were bathed in your light.
Your grace enkindled love in our hearts,
and we awoke to our ignorance.

Knowing our sins, we knelt in humility
to beg your forgiveness.
In your infinite mercy, you forgave us,
and saved us from final self-destruction.

Even the best of human wisdom fades
in the absence of perfect faith.
But as your love filled our souls,
the clouds dispersed.
Trust and goodness returned to our hearts.

Our faith strengthened by your love,
we reach out to those in distress
with the light of Johrei.
We will build Paradise on Earth,
the land of the divine will.

For your boundless love, O Lord,
we are forever grateful.
Your mercy flows out to all humankind,
even the most sinful prisoners of evil.

The blessings you have vouchsafed us
are too numerous, too vast to fathom.
Unworthy as we are,
we thank you, God.

Judgment

Lord, you rule the universe
with compassion and wisdom.
In your mercy you have revealed to us
the end of this world approaching.

From the bitter sceptic and haughty tyrant,
to the humble servant of deep faith,
all will prostrate themselves
before the throne of judgment.

Like a woman in labor,
the world is struggling in anguish
to give birth to a new kingdom.
The last day is soon upon us.

There is but one way, O God.
May your grace fill us all.
Embrace our penitent hearts
and grant forgiveness of our sins.

Let us not dwell in eternal darkness.
Judge us as good, deem us
worthy to stand in your presence
and serve you with the light of Johrei.

Sickness

Almighty God, Creator of all things,
healer of all distress,
without your grace we are helpless.

Sickness shows us how weak we are
    without your guiding hand.
But we bear its pain, for we know
it is a sign of purification.

We give thanks for the blessings
    of purification;
it is a gift from you that leads us
to the gate of eternal life.

Striving to fulfill the sacred mission
    you gave us,
we are your faithful servants,
who are to build a world without sickness.

Help us, O God;
in your love, help us in our search
for oneness with you.

Sacred Mission

Almighty God, in your unfathomable wisdom,
you showed us the road to salvation.

How vulnerable we are without
    your protection.
Plagued are we by sin and suffering.

You taught us to give ourselves fully
    into your hands.
Your spirit guides us through our lives.

In our weakness, help us to follow
    your commandments.
Only then can we be just and true.

Enlighten our soul, O Lord,
and strengthen our will;
that we may strive harder to
    help our neighbors,
bringing them the divine light of Johrei.

Enlighten our soul, O Lord,
and fill us with your spirit;
that our hearts may be selfless,
    our acts good,
our lives devoted to others.

Enlighten our soul, O Lord,
and bless us with your grace;
that we may carry on our service of love
    and charity,
with the divine light of Johrei.

Purification

O God, you who are eternal life,
even in my sin you have let me share
the purifying power of Johrei.
Penitent and forgiven,
I will strive to fill my life
with thoughts and acts of love.

Let my body and spirit be cleansed,
my soul illuminated by your love,
and fused with your will.
My whole being yearns to hear your voice
speaking of love and truth.
Cleansed of all that offends you,
I stand before only you as judge.

I commit myself totally to the sacred mission
of serving you and helping my companions
throughout the world.

When the solemn moment of judgment comes,
blessed is the one who embraces you
in his purified, innermost self.

In awe of your divine grace,
I give unending prayers
for ultimate unity with you.

Healing

Almighty God, you gave us
the saving light of Johrei, the life-giving energy
that is the hope of the world.

Your divine power is the only power
that can restore when life is waning.
Johrei, your gift to us,
is a sacred treasure for humankind.

Our mission is the blessed work
of healing by your divine light.
Inspired by your love for all people,
we are strengthened to fulfill your command.
Purify the souls of the wicked, O Lord,
let them bathe in the light of Johrei,

for they will repent of their sins,
and walk the path to true humanity.

Greater than the deepest ocean is
the magnitude of your mercy.
Your light in Johrei cleanses
the filth and evil of this world.

With each day, each minute,
the spiritual world grows brighter,
invisible, yet everywhere,
heralding the coming of Paradise on Earth.

We will dedicate ourselves to you,
and build your kingdom in this world.

In Praise of Creation

O God, creator of heaven and earth,
you gave the human soul love,
that it may respond to your call.
You gave us flesh and mind, limbs and senses,
that we may serve your purposes.
Lord of creation, you made a delightful abode
    of peace
for hearts purified of clouds to enjoy.
We see flowers brightening the spring meadows,
and we hear birds calling on the mountain
    in summer.
Our hearts dance with the brilliance
    of the autumn leaves
and find repose in winter's white tranquility.
The birds and flowers, wind and moon,
are friends to lighten our sojourn in this world.
O Lord, great God, you made them all.
Mother Nature declares the beauty
    of your works,
the bounty of your blessings,
and the boundlessness of your love.

Raging billows soar heavenward
and sweep over offshore isles.
Surging waves crash against rugged cliffs
and swallow unwary rocks in their wake.

Once the storm calms,
serenity returns to the sea.
Rippling waters glisten in the sunlight,
slapping foam along the beach.
Small fishing boats dart in and out
among the isles in the offing.
The placid sea brings peace of mind;
its endless depths echo the infinity
   of your grace.

Spring adorns the mountains with blossoms,
summer decorates them with youthful green.
Puffy clouds float over the summit,
the mist comes and goes
before it settles, damp, on the hillsides.
Against a crisp autumn sky,
the mountains stand in bold relief,
coated with tinted leaves.
Unblemished white covers wintery peaks,
their rocky folds reflecting the sunlight.
The beauty of the mountains vibrates
with the rhythm of the seasons.
Their streams, trees, and grasses are all
the fruit of your divine craftsmanship.

Shimmering heat dances in the air
to the patter of thawing snow in the wilderness.
Butterflies make their rendezvous
in meadows resplendent with color.

As the summer grass turns brown,
the flowers of fall come into their own,
and the air is aflutter with dragonflies.
A benign moon warms the deep sky,
and insects sing their elegies in the field;
the late autumn balm for a poetic mind.

A half moon slides out of the mountain ridge,
brightening the villages below.
The light of a full moon bounces
off glassy water;
a waning moon sends shining arrows
dodging through the surf.
Dawn climbers ascend, heading toward
a fading moon lingering over the peak.
A lonely soul wanders through the dusk,
the moon rising over the farthest corner
    of the field.
A troubled mind gazes
at the silver disc approaching its zenith.
No matter its shape,
or where one happens to be,
the moon brings solace and
healing for spiritual wounds.

The fields and hills are a kaleidoscope
of flowering plants through the changing seasons.
All are divine gifts.
A plum orchard creates a landscape
of black and white under a hazy vernal moon.
Cherry trees parade their lacy flounce of low,

fleecy blossoms along the riverbank.
Camellias in full bloom
stain the garden red, pink, and white.
A brocade of summer azaleas ornaments
rocks in alpine ridges.

Refreshing hues of morning glory
greet the dawn of a hot summer day.
Hagi, bellflowers, and arrowroots
create an autumn palette in the meadow.
All are your creation for man to appreciate.
All are manifestations of your heavenly love.
O Lord, we love the beauty of the plants
and flowers you created for us.

We praise the wonder of your works.
We marvel at the beauty of your world.
Of all things in your great universe,
we rejoice in your wonderful power of creation
that gives us beauty, love, and life.

The Blessings of God

O Lord, giver of all blessings,
unsurpassed in the power of your love,
your unseen hand does all things.
You have brought us the joy of new vision,
awakening us to see that we are nothing
without your grace and protection.
The vastness of your bounty
surpasses human understanding.
Unceasing are your blessings as you help us,
small and weak in our sin,
to build Paradise on Earth.

You fill us with your power and
our armor is the sword of your truth;
we will not fear contempt or hardship.
Those who receive your grace
ride calm and secure through all upheavals,
protected by the blessings of Johrei.
We entrust our body and soul to you, O Lord,
we give ourselves to become
the vehicle of your providence.
We devote ourselves to helping humankind
in our sacred mission on earth.

We kneel before you, O Lord of compassion,
who saves the sinful,
in humble, grateful thanks.

For Repose

O God, revered Lord of eternal love,
you are the fount of our salvation.
In the midst of our unhappiness,
you showed us the joy of leading others
    out of distress
through the divine power of Johrei.
Who can be more perfectly blessed
than he who has a vision of encounter
with the divine!

Whatever catastrophes befall,
we will walk firmly in the path
    you laid for us.
Strengthened by your grace,
our hearts are filled with gladness
when you bring peace and salvation
to our innermost being.

We, who know the joy in building
    Paradise on Earth,
pray for the many who know only the misery
of ceaseless strife
because they do not know you.
We offer ourselves to you, O God,
that we may live in the happiness of repose,
no matter how humble our houses
or simple our lives.

Great God, who gave us life,
we will faithfully abide by your will
and give all our strength to the sacred work
     of Johrei.
We will tell all the world the joyful news
that you are with us.

O Lord, reach out in your mercy
even to those who oppose your will.
Our very existence depends
on the great might of your love.
You have restored us, O Lord,
you have given us new life
that we may serve you.

Prayer for the Blind

Blinded by sin we wander in darkness,
unable to find the light of truth.
Ignorant of your presence in our hearts,
we continue in our evil ways
until our souls are in agony,
clouded by the sin of unbelief.
O Lord, open our eyes and let us see.

Sinful are we who fail to see
the bountiful works of God.
Pitiful are we who value only
what we can touch and feel
and do not prize the soul.
When, finally, after a long nightmare,
our souls are bathed in Johrei's light,
we will be awakened to the truth.
O Lord, open our eyes and let us see.

Blessed are we who overcome
our selfish attachments
to give ourselves in love to serve others.
The clouds will be lifted from our souls.
We at last will see God in our hearts.
We lift our voices in praise, O God,
for you are always with us.

Wedding Prayer

O God of profound mercy, in your great love,
you have willed that these two be joined together.
With your grace, two are made as one,
vowing to stay together to the end.

With hearts joined in unity,
together they will meet all trials and hardships,
together they will walk in the path of goodness
through the years
until white crowns their heads.

Faithfully they will follow your will
and purify their lives with Johrei.
Whatever obstacles loom ahead, these two
will overcome them in their love for each other,
and they will praise you more with each passing day.

From this day onward, O God,
help these two as they pledge their strength together
to build on this earth your paradise,
and bring them true happiness in their sacred travail.

Prayer for the Dead

. O Lord, our savior,
in your infinite mercy
grant the remission of all his/her sins
to the soul of [   ],
who has departed this world.

Grant him/her your grace
that he/she may enter the gate of heaven.
May the departed soul find eternal solace
in the realm of the spirit,
where divine justice is complete.

Let the wonderful light of Johrei
shine forth in its purifying power
to save all souls from hell's damnation.

May this departed soul know salvation
in the realm of the spirit
and find never-ending joy
in union with the divine.
Hear our prayer, O Lord.

Part Four
LIFE AND THOUGHT OF MOKICHI OKADA

A Brief Biography

Born in 1882 into the family of a small shopkeeper in downtown Tokyo, Mokichi Okada was raised in the earthy and pious environment of the urban entrepreneurial class. His parents belonged to a temple dedicated to Kannon, the Buddhist deity of mercy, but their observances seem to have been simple and practical, and not particularly appealing to their son. During his youth, Mr. Okada had no direct involvement with religious affairs, and certainly no healing experience. His activities as a religious leader did not begin until middle age, after he felt himself called by God to perform a specific mission in the world. Nothing in his childhood even suggested such an event; in fact, he was distinctly uninterested in religion for many years.

He later reminisced, "I never really believed in Kannon," but from an early age he demonstrated a deep desire to help people. He often gave donations to the Salvation Army and other charities, "not because I had any faith, but because I enjoyed sharing the work these groups did for society." His concern for the welfare of others was intense and he developed a sense of justice that was to color his thinking and teaching throughout the rest of his life. Underhanded, corrupt, and dishonest behavior were abhorrent to him, especially in politicians or anyone in a position of leadership or responsibility.

From his childhood, our founder, who loved art, aspired to be a painter. When an eye disease forced him to abandon that dream, he turned to business. By 1916 he had built up an adequate financial base on which he wanted to found a newspaper and use it as his mouthpiece to protest the wrongs he saw around him. To secure enough capital for the venture, he started a finance company in 1918. He was deeply discouraged when the failure of his main bank led his firm into bankruptcy the following year. In February 1920 he incorporated a new company, but that, too, was wiped out after only one month when a major panic created havoc in the Japanese economy. On top of his wife's death the year before, two successive business failures left him depressed and disheartened. He struggled to pick up again and he remarried. He was just beginning to build a new base for his life and his business when the Great Kanto Earthquake of 1923 struck, ruining Mr. Okada along with thousands of others.

The earthquake was a turning point. Having reached the age of forty-one, Mr. Okada began to question the meaning of human life and destiny, and to ponder the possibility of salvation. He finally decided to seek some kind of answer in religion, and later that year he joined Ōmotokyō, a world renewal religion with a syncretic

Shinto base founded in 1892 by Nao Deguchi (1837–1918).

Beginning of Renewal

Mr. Okada began to meditate frequently, and this may be about when he became aware of the existence in his life of a powerful, otherworldly force that his deepening involvement in Ōmotokyō seemed to confirm. In his personal quest for the relationship between that force and man, the specific teachings of Ōmotokyō had less impact on Mr. Okada than the experience of prayer. Soon after he became a member, he began to realize that through prayer he could help people suffering from illness. To him, this was the greatest blessing imaginable. Supported by constant meditation and growing certainty of a supreme being, he pushed onward to learn more about the nature of this being he sensed. "During that time," he wrote of those months of immersion in religious thought, "something was moving me at will; by some miracle it was leading me little by little to know a divine world. I was so happy then, I couldn't keep my joy from just bursting out."

In 1926, Mr. Okada received a series of revelations. The first ones were communicated to him by Kannon, who identified the source of the revelations as God. Mr. Okada said about the first revelation:

At about midnight one night in 1926, the most peculiar sensation came over me, a feeling I had never experienced before. It was an overwhelming urge that I simply cannot describe; I had an irresistible compulsion to talk. There was no way to suppress the power that was using my voice. So I gave in. The first words were, "Get something to write with." Just as soon as my wife brought paper and pen, a torrent was let loose.

His idea of God crystallized out of what was revealed to him. The divinity in Ōmotokyō is explained by a complex set of ideas that posit many heterogeneous deities, but the revelations convinced Mr. Okada that there is only one God, Creator of the universe, who made man to heed His will. He is the God of love and salvation, reaching out to lift man from the unhappy, sinful state of rebellion against Him. Mr. Okada learned that God ordains man to build Paradise on Earth. "The great mission of building Paradise on Earth was made known to me at that time. I didn't believe it at first, but then too many miracles happened," Mr. Okada wrote. "They compelled me to believe." For a time he remained indecisive and quiet about the revelations. He did not speak of God's command that he tell people of the coming of Paradise on Earth and heal the sick. "It dawned on me only slowly what a stupendous mission God had given me," Mr. Okada admitted.

Independent Church and Johrei

His awareness of that mission seemed to increase the personal warmth and sympathy he felt for others. In the meantime, Mr. Okada's powerful charisma and the mind-numbing instances of restoration and recovery that were occurring through his healing were attracting a fast-growing group of personal followers. It was only a matter of time before his leadership qualities became apparent and he was put in charge of a temple in Tokyo. From there, however, his work moved into a dimension that was quite different from the mainstream. At the time, the sect was still narrowly culture-bound and nationalistic; Western dress and Western food were prohibited, among other restrictions. But contemporary reports attest that Mr. Okada's guidance was realistic and liberal, and demonstrated practical concerns.

Mr. Okada did not get involved in political or ideological movements within the sect. He immersed himself wholly in helping the suffering, and teaching others the meaning of religious faith and what it involves. He was first and foremost a teacher, and remained so throughout his life. He lived out his belief in human equality, always able to meet others on their terms and always inspiring complete trust. When he began regular healing activities in 1928, people gravitated naturally to him for help and advice.

Mr. Okada's unorthodoxy and his increasing personal following within Ōmotokyō generated antagonism, particularly among the leaders. In the tense atmosphere of the early 1930s, any kind of extremism had fertile ground. Some fanatics within the sect were so strongly against his activities that Mr. Okada grew uneasy, for their attacks were directed as much at his followers as himself. In 1934, his position untenable by then, Mr.

Okada left Ōmotokyō and founded a new organization. Eight years had elapsed since the first revelations in 1926. During that time, Mr. Okada had thought a great deal about forming an independent group, but until he felt absolutely certain that his work could best be done apart from the sect he had served for so long, he did not make the actual decision. To break away was probably the only way he could continue to minister to the several hundred followers who stayed with him, and whose ranks were augmented by many who joined later.

The new group was dedicated to spreading the message revealed by God, and it was free of the doctrinal and behavioral strictures of Ōmotokyō. Soon after breaking away, he established a service of worship and prayer for the new church. In January 1935 it received a name: the Greater Japan Society of Kannon. There were several reasons for using "Kannon." One was political; any overt suggestion in the name or otherwise that his healing power came from God, would be tantamount to asserting power equal to, or greater than, the power of the emperor, who was considered a "living god" at the time. The church would be open to criminal charges of lese majesty and possibly prosecuted.

Most important, Kannon is familiar to Japanese. This was crucial, for Mr. Okada had to be very careful to begin his teaching simply, in ways people could understand. There was nothing in Japan's religious traditions to help them understand the existence of one, and only one God, who loves all people. Kannon, however, could be seen as God's deputy, a communicator in making known God's will on earth. For that reason "Kannon" was retained in the name when the church was reinstated in August 1947.

Mr. Okada used the phrase "blessings of Kannon" for the next fifteen years in explaining the idea of God's love and the need for repentance. Finally, in 1950, the group was reorganized as Sekai Meshiakyō [Church of World Messianity], and from then on virtually all reference to Kannon in Mr. Okada's writing ceased.

The founder's discussions on the nature of God and His acts in the world apparently were derived from the revelations. An analysis of his teachings to determine exactly what Mr. Okada learned in the first revelations indicate four main points: (1) God asks man to repent; (2) man is entrusted by God with the sacred task of building a world of truth, goodness, and beauty; (3) those who fail to repent will be punished at the judgment; and (4) Mokichi Okada is commanded to convey these things to all people.

For the first several years of his healing ministry, Mr. Okada depended only on prayer. Then in 1935, he learned of Johrei through revelation, and it proved to be incomparably more powerful. He relates that soon after the establishment of the Society of Kannon the same year, God inspired him to make seals for each of his followers to help them in their healing activities. Mr. Okada took pieces of paper and wrote the character for "light" on them. The seal helped the bearer to transmit the divine light to the sick, giving him the assurance that he was not alone as he prayed to God. This was the first time Johrei was known in the world. Johrei not only drew throngs of people to be healed and to witness healing, but more, enabled many to fully accept the existence of God. Thus, during the 1930s, even in the face of growing pressure from a government moving towards war and national repression, the number of his followers steadily grew.

War and the Aftermath

Around 1936 measures that would soon bring almost every aspect of national and individual life under control of the military began to strangle the life of churches and religious groups of all kinds. The new religions, including Ōmotokyō, were treated particularly harshly. For the Society of Kannon, the first big blow was the prohibition of all healing under the sponsorship of a religious group. In response to that, Mr. Okada ceased all religious teaching activities. He kept the group together by continuing to practice Johrei everywhere possible and teaching others how to administer it. It was also during the mid-thirties that he began practicing nature farming to demonstrate the truth of the God-inspired method of cultivation.

Until about 1943, most of his disciples lived and worked in Tokyo, with the exception of a very few who went into the local regions to hold seminars, heal, and teach the channeling of Johrei. But once the bombing of Tokyo intensified in June 1944, much of the population was evacuated to the countryside, Mr. Okada's disciples among them. As it turned out, however, this forced relocation became an opportunity to introduce Johrei to people in local regions who otherwise might not have been reached so easily. The other, perversely positive result of the bombing was the chance it gave people, especially in Tokyo, to see the work of Johrei through the ministry of Mr. Okada and his disciples in healing the injured and protecting those yet unharmed. Of twenty followers who were in Hiroshima city when the A-bomb was dropped, not one was killed. All of them wore a seal, a piece of paper with the character for "light" written on it.

After the war was over, new horizons opened up for Japan's religions. All restrictions were lifted and freedom of belief was guaranteed under the new Constitution. Mr. Okada's group was recognized as more than just a healing society and allowed to incorporate as a religious organization.

The central precept of the faith that Mr. Okada taught is that man will participate in building Paradise on Earth, which the healing power of Johrei can help him attain. Mr. Okada also taught that the beauty of nature and the creative arts exert an elevating influence on the soul. While he stressed spiritual and physical health as the essential condition that enables a person to carry out his or her mission in life, he constantly noted the importance of beauty in one's daily surroundings.

Mr. Okada bought land during the war in Hakone and Atami with the intention of building places of inspiration, places where esthetic values would dominate.

After the war he had gardens constructed in both, according to his own plans, and in 1952 a museum was completed in the Hakone garden. There he placed a large number of works, which he sought out and in many cases rescued from obscurity. Today these works are considered priceless treasures. The collection that grew there contains masterpieces of Japanese art, including paintings by Ogata Kōrin and Sōtatsu, calligraphy and lacquerware by Hon'ami Kōetsu, ceramics made by Ninsei and Ogata Kenzan, among others. There are also some Chinese and Korean masterpieces. All of them reflect the fine artistic taste of Mr. Okada, himself a sensitive painter and master of calligraphy, design, flower arranging, and tea ceremony, as well as poet and connoisseur of ceramics.

The collection he assembled is a priceless treasure of art, and it is one of Japan's best. In late 1981 a second large museum was completed in Atami to make the entire collection more accessible to the public. While the Hakone Museum focuses on ceramics and porcelains, the new museum houses most of the paintings collected by Mr. Okada, in addition to some acquired later by his successors.

Teacher and Pastor

Mr. Okada took care to prevent the kind of adulation that could develop into a cult. Those who knew him describe very definite charismatic qualities in his leadership, but they derived from the love, humility, simplicity, and warmth of the man. He personally answered every letter that came to his attention, and often his letters alone were able to help people he had never even met. He had a prodigious memory for the individual circumstances of people and was constantly checking on the progress of the sick, advising, and giving counsel.

One instance of his never-ceasing concern occurred just before the end of the war. A woman, whose spinal condition had been helped previously by Johrei after fifteen years of bed-ridden immobility, unexpectedly became paralyzed in her lower body and she could not walk. She happened to be particularly active in serving others. Mr. Okada learned of this, and telephoned her, telling her to come as soon as possible from her home in Yokosuka to Atami for treatment. It was 1945, and almost impossible to find a car, and she was unable to take a train. She also didn't realize—as Mr. Okada did—how serious her condition was. The worry apparent in his constant telephone calls moved her to pray fervently for a car to get her there. The next day she found a car for hire to make the trip, and under Mr. Okada's care she recovered.

Many people still remember a meeting that took place in 1943. A large group had gathered, including high-ranking officers and business executives. It was wartime, and Mr. Okada was under proscription not to preach or teach religious precepts. Regardless, when a lone high school student stood up and began to fire questions about the theological meaning of Johrei, Mr. Okada's replies were straightforward, containing no condescension. He treated the boy as an intelligent, equal adult, and answered in as much depth as the youth could handle at that time.

The years before and during the war represented a special trial for Mr. Okada, who was forced to cease so much of his activity by the authorities. Unable to practice healing openly as a religious leader, he had to carry on partially and covertly. After the war, when people were free to profess religious affiliations, church membership rapidly multiplied. Many new buildings and facilities were needed, and this imposed a different kind of constraint. For several years the demanding job of planning alone made it impossible for Mr. Okada to carry on pastoral work full time.

Postwar Developments

Organizationally also, the religion underwent change after the war. Under its first postwar restructure in 1947, the Japan Kannon Church was established with eight churches, each led by one of Mr. Okada's closest disciples. The Miroku Church was by far the biggest, having a membership larger than all the other seven combined. This church became legally independent in 1948 under the name Nihon Miroku Kyōkai. In 1950 the religion was renamed Sekai Meshiakyō, and all churches were reunited under the formal leadership of Mr. Okada. At first the whole membership was divided into three large groups, but they turned out to be unwieldy and hard to administer. The following year, eighty separate churches were set up, each one directly supervised by the main church under Mr. Okada.

On his sixty-eighth birthday, December 23, 1950, Mr. Okada announced his plan to write "Birth of the New Civilization" as a definitive statement on the theory and practice of Johrei. In 1953, two churches were established in the United States in an effort to begin propagating the faith throughout all nations.

When Mr. Okada died in 1955, he was seventy-two. There were tens of thousands at his funeral, a tremendous tribute to a man who had done so much to help people. The church, however, was not adequately prepared for his passing. Most of the members had not yet attained a deep enough understanding of Mr. Okada's teachings to be able to carry on. His followers had all practiced Johrei, had all experienced its blessings firsthand, and had saved innumerable seriously ill people from vegetation or death. That experience, however, caused many to regard Johrei as the means *and* the end of the faith. They failed to study Mr. Okada's teachings systematically, and as a result their understanding of the basic tenets of their faith remained vague, at best.

After Mr. Okada's death, his widow succeeded him, as is customary in Japanese religious groups. Soon thereafter, Mrs. Okada began to lead the church in a new direction in an attempt to provide clear, solid leadership. In so doing, however, she introduced her own ideas into her ministry, many of which were adapted from Ōmotokyō. She refused to pass on many of her late husband's teachings and even withheld a large number of his tracts. For one reason or another, most of the disciples accepted her revisions of the doctrine. The church as a whole began to deviate sharply from the basic principles and practice that Mr. Okada had established, as became apparent a few years later.

In such circumstances it proved to be almost impossible to maintain the teaching Mr. Okada had begun, and this prompted several disciples to join together in an earnest effort to seek out and preserve the original teachings as they appear in his articles, sermons, and speeches. Eventually some of those disciples who were truly committed to their mentor's doctrine broke away, establishing their own independent churches. Their organizations have expanded and served thousands of new members over the years since they began their work to preserve the integrity of the faith.

Bibliographical Notes

1 General

The works of Mokichi Okada range over every major field, from religion and culture to natural and social science. They include about forty complete volumes, several of which have never been published. One of those manuscripts is "Birth of the New Civilization," which forms the core of this English-language volume. Mr. Okada also wrote about three thousand articles that appeared in newspapers and periodicals.[28-31] In addition, the transcriptions of his sermons, talks, and question-answer sessions with disciples and believers make up eighty-two entire volumes.[18-20] His written work is considerably more polished in style and organization than the transcriptions of oral material, but the content of the latter is often very informative and sophisticated. Finally, Mr. Okada is the author of about four thousand poems.

A strong religious outlook runs through all of Mr. Okada's writing, no matter what the subject; in all his essays and talks he makes it clear that God is one, and

God is creator of the universe. A major problem, however, is that in much of his writing, Mr. Okada was constrained by the need to make basic principles clear to people for whom this kind of faith was totally new, and he often left points only partially developed to avoid confusing them. The first generation of Japanese believers had few cultural or intellectual precedents to help them understand his teaching, and as a result, much of what he said may appear to be oversimplified. But those whose faith became firm and deep under Mr. Okada's guidance can, with their greater knowledge, now reread these writings and find much more meaning in them than they did decades ago.

The transcriptions of his talks and conversations were made as he spoke, and since they tend to contain ad hoc material added as he went along, they are harder to organize and analyze than his essays. The records of his conversations also contain references to subjects that he did not discuss in articles, such as the substance of the revelations, and the more profound aspects of God's will and providence. Some of his closest disciples later studied all of Mr. Okada's oral presentations. They divided them into categories by subject matter, for convenience in teaching the elements of the faith, and they produced several types of supplementary aids in mimeographed form.[21–27] Nevertheless, much more research on the materials is needed in order to present clearly the full message they contain.

2 Treatises on Religion

Mr. Okada's voluminous writings on religious subjects generally can be divided into four categories. Those in the first category deal with topics that are of common interest and are comprehensible to lay believers with little knowledge of religion, especially monotheistic systems of belief. This category also includes treatises for beginners in the faith written to guide them in everyday conduct and practice. *Essays on Faith*[3] is an introduction to the basic doctrine, written in plain language for the interested public shortly after the Japan Kannon Church was legally incorporated as a religious organization in 1947. Works in this category comprise almost one-half of all the religious treatises written by Mr. Okada.

The second category covers his writing on the realm of spirit and spiritual experiences in human life. *Glimpses into the Spiritual World*[4] is the most systematic treatment of the topic. Although it is based primarily on inspiration, the book includes analyses of utterances made, during the administration of Johrei, by spirits possessing the recipients. It also touches upon some of the special diseases caused by possession. In the third category are general discussions of religious doctrine, centering on such familiar concepts as truth, happiness, good and evil. These were written at different times primarily for the purpose of propagating the faith in Japanese society. One of these is *An Introduction to Sekai Meshiakyō*,[11] which describes the historical role of the church and some of the key concepts in the faith. Together, the books and articles in categories two and three make up more than two-fifths of all Mr. Okada's writing on religion. Works in the fourth category, which constitute less than ten percent, deal with the end of this world and the judgment that will come before the advent of Paradise on Earth.

Essays on Religion[16] is a collection of magazine and newspaper articles written by Mr. Okada before July 1953. Compiled by Ichiro Nakamura and published by the church headquarters with the author's endorsement, the volume encompasses all of the four categories mentioned above. Mr. Okada's verbal statements on religious doctrine are contained in *Sin*[26] and *On Ideas*,[27] which were also compiled by Rev. Nakamura. Similarly, *Guide to Ministry*,[21] *Johrei*,[22] *Ministry of Healing*,[25] *Belief*,[24] *Sacred Service*,[23] and others were compiled as pastoral aids.

Another group of predominantly religious writings, possibly a fifth category, are the autobiographical essays. *Stories of Miracles*[6] describes major religious events in Mr. Okada's life, including the series of divine revelations he received in 1926. That volume is supplemented by a number of testimonies written by his followers. *The Pathway to Light*[8] is an autobiographical sketch covering the thirty-year period from 1919 to 1949. It explains the set of circumstances that led Mr. Okada to seek answers in religion and describes the manner in which he received God's revelations; his difficult prewar ministry of healing, carried out under the pressure of strict police surveillance; and the hardships and persecution he underwent during and after the war. This volume in particular shows the author to have been a man with a broad interest in human affairs that ranged from politics and economics to the arts and education, not to speak of science and religion.

It is possible to classify Mr. Okada's religious writings in this way, but that does not mean that his thoughts on the key doctrinal concepts are systematically presented in them. In fact, only a few articles concentrate on the ideas vital to the religion. Such expositions are scattered, often buried deep in longer treatises, unedited transcripts of sermons and lectures, or even in poems and prayers. Mr. Okada's thinking on basic issues does not become fully clear, therefore, until his work is carefully indexed and his numerous comments on and references to God and other concepts are collated and arranged in logical sequence.

Mr. Okada tried to teach in graduated steps, advancing at the same pace with the growing understanding achieved by his followers. Rather than forcing them to struggle with difficult concepts from the start, he tried to explain God and His works in as plain and concrete terms as possible. A good example of this approach is in *God Works Miracles*,[15] which attempts to bring out the spiritual meaning of miracles by commenting on testimonies written by beneficiaries and administrators of Johrei. Some of these people were in Hiroshima or Nagasaki in the summer of 1945. They not only survived, but went on to help many victims of the bomb with Johrei.

It was not until his final years that he began writing more systematically about the deeper levels of the faith.

"Birth of the New Civilization" was the first, and unfortunately the only, fruit of such efforts. Based on divine revelation, it was written to inform people of the misapprehensions on which our present civilization is built, and to announce God's message for the reform of the world. Mr. Okada stipulated that this work be translated and conveyed to the people of every nation. He was going to write "An Anatomy of Divine Spirituality" as a sequel to "Birth." If he had lived longer, that work would have been his definitive teaching on God and His providence.

3   Critiques on Civilization

Mr. Okada's writing on the history and character of human civilizations reflects his eschatological vision for this world. He believed any civilization that did not develop ways to resolve the problems of sickness, poverty, and war could never be called genuine. Modern man in particular has increased his misery by relying too heavily on material values, on science and technology. Unless we recognize the fundamental flaws in our civilization and change its course, he wrote, it might turn out to be the agent of our very destruction.

Our world, plagued as it is by war, poverty and sickness, is nearing a dead end. Mr. Okada saw the final judgment as imminent; if man repents he will be saved, but if he fails to repent, he is doomed to perish.

Mr. Okada wrote no single volume devoted exclusively to the problems of civilization, although "Birth of the New Civilization" came close to being a comprehensive work on the subject. He originally intended to include chapters on politics, economics and society, and elaborate on the question of war and peace. But he passed away before he could complete it.

Critiques of specific social, political, or economic issues abound in the form of magazine or newspaper essays and transcriptions of public speeches. Many of these have been put together in part two of a volume compiled by his disciples under the title, *Essays on Art and Society*.[17] Part 5 of *Essays on Religion*[16] also contains fifteen critical articles on contemporary civilization with a focus on Japanese culture.

These essays were Mr. Okada's mouthpiece in his condemnation of social injustice, political corruption, totalitarianism, militarism, and power politics. An advocate of world government, he urged that leaders of every country "free themselves and turn instead to plan for the well-being of all mankind." He also analyzed the causes of poverty, inflation, bankruptcy, crime, suicide, and a host of other social and economic problems, and offered a prescription for deep-reaching, permanent reform.

As the cold war intensified, Mr. Okada wrote many articles denouncing the policies of the Soviet Union. He attacked Stalinism and international communism with particularly passionate fervor. He saw in the United States a Christian nation and also the liberator of Japan; he believed that nation embodied many of the values he was trying to instill, even though it leaned too far towards materialism. Interestingly enough, he predicted the Sino-Soviet rift and Sino-American rapprochement as early as the Korean War years. As he put it, "Mao Tse-tung and Chou En-lai are both wise men. Someday they are going to astound the whole world by suddenly turning against the Russians and shaking hands with the Americans."

4   Johrei and Nature Farming

During the years between 1935 and the end of World War II in 1945, Mr. Okada spoke and preached on Johrei and subjects related to disease and health, but writing, and religious or intellectual expressions of any kind, were heavily censored in Japan during that period. Since it was almost impossible to publish, today all we have from that time is a small number of treatises that were originally delivered as lectures and were recorded by some of Mr. Okada's followers. At one point in 1942–43 the church managed to get into print a three-volume tract, *Medicine for Tomorrow*[1] (for distribution only among believers), but a few months later it was censored and pulled out of circulation.

One of the first things Mr. Okada did after the war was over, and freedom of belief, speech, and expression was guaranteed, was to revise the three volumes of *Medicine for Tomorrow*. The second edition was published in one volume in 1947 as *The Gospels of Heaven*.[2] The first half in particular contains concrete, detailed discussions on the need to reconsider the conventional attitudes towards disease and healing, as well as on how we should proceed from here. Now, even after almost four decades, some concepts and observations in this work stand out as truly remarkable in their insight and perceptiveness.

Mr. Okada published a large number of articles and short essays on disease and Johrei in the church newspapers[28 – 30] and magazines.[31] They were written primarily for believers, but they also attracted a wider readership by virtue of their timeliness and relevance to current topics and issues. *A Divinely-inspired Approach to Health*[10] is one of the many essay collections compiled by Mr. Okada himself.

Several original works were published in the early 1950s for the general public. *Spiritual Healing of Tuberculosis*[14] is an example. TB was still the top killer in Japan at that time, hence Mr. Okada devoted much of his writing to that particular ailment. He predicted, however, that even though cases of tuberculosis might be reduced considerably, it would be replaced by increasingly complex, intractable diseases, including cancer.

One of the most definitive works on Johrei is "Birth of the New Civilization." This important work, the core of which is presented in English in this volume, places the concept of purification and the spiritual and physical meaning of Johrei within a broad theoretical framework.

Most of Mr. Okada's articles on nature farming appeared in the church newspapers. *Notes on Nature Farming*,[12] especially the revised and enlarged edition of 1953, contains articles and case studies selected by Mr. Okada and is the most important exposition of his views on the subject.

Like his pronouncements on religion, Mr. Okada's statements on healing, disease, nutrition, and nature farming are also scattered in his speeches and lectures, records of question-and-answer sessions, and transcriptions of interviews by scholars and journalists. For a fuller and deeper understanding of his thinking on these more practical topics, therefore, it will be necessary to collate all the fragmentary pieces and carry out a rigorous, systematic analysis of them as a whole.

5 The Arts

Mr. Okada attached great importance to art and in the church periodicals wrote almost sixty articles on esthetics and individual artistic masterpieces. *Assorted Reflections*[5] is a collection of twenty-one essays that were selected by the author himself, while part one of *Essays on Art and Society*[17] is a posthumous collection of Mr. Okada's articles on art and culture.

Outstanding works of art created by artists whose souls are pure, Mr. Okada taught, can serve as a vehicle of spiritual elevation for anyone who appreciates them. Artists in the various genres, including literature, the fine arts, music, drama, dance, and film-making, must have a certain nobility of character and always strive to purify their souls in order to be able to guide other people to truth, goodness, and beauty through their creative activities. It was with this conviction in mind that Mr. Okada wrote many critical essays on Eastern and Western art.

A large number of articles are devoted to discussions

of the outstanding Japanese artists and their masterpieces. In Mr. Okada's view, the greatest painter in Japanese history was Ogata Kōrin (1638–1716), whose "Red and White Plum Trees" is without parallel in its masterful, intuitive representation of the motif. The founder also praised the craftsmanship of Hon'ami Kōetsu (1558–1637) and paintings by Sōtatsu (17th century). Among the ceramists, Mr. Okada held Ogata Kenzan (1663–1743) and Ninsei (17th century) in high esteem. He regarded the latter's "Wisteria Jar" as the best among Japanese works in pottery.

6 Hymns and Poetry

The core collection of Mr. Okada's poetry is a series of verses celebrating the faith, chiefly hymns.[13] He also wrote poems in praise of God, and he published two other anthologies of poetry under his pen name, Akemaro: *Selected Poems of Akemaro*[7] contains chiefly lyrical poems, and *Mountain and Stream*[9] focuses on the beauty of nature. Finally there are poems published in newspapers and periodicals. Mr. Okada's poems are a source of enlightenment for believers, for they often encapsulate and highlight the most important religious truths.

Selected Publications

The list below represents only a part of Mr. Okada's voluminous writing. The publications cited above are arranged in chronological order within each category. Numbers 4–8 and 10 in the first category were published as a series of booklets called *Jikan sōsho*. "Jikan" (literally, "self-contemplation") was one of Mr. Okada's pen names. Jikan appears as the author of nos. 4–6, 8, and 10–12, while Akemaro is used in all of his poetry volumes, namely, nos. 7, 9, and 13. His real name is used in all the other books, except for nos. 16 and 17, which were edited by the Department of Doctrinal Studies of the church headquarters.

The volumes in category two are all transcriptions of Mr. Okada's lectures, sermons, and conversations with his disciples, compiled chronologically by the church headquarters. Numbers 19 and 20 cover roughly the same period, but they differ widely in content: whereas the former volumes are records of question-and-answer sessions with close disciples, the latter contain teachings transmitted orally to local church leaders and lay believers.

Those in the third category also include transcriptions of oral teachings, but they center on particular topics or themes, which are evident in their titles. Seikō Kyōkai is the predecessor of Light of Salvation Church, of which Ichiro Nakamura is director.

It is impractical to try to list here all the articles Mr. Okada wrote for the church publications. Let it suffice to give some information on the periodicals in which his essays originally appeared. Numbers 28–30 are the same weekly newspaper, but its name was changed twice. Number 31 is a magazine. Both *Eikō* [Glory] and *Chijō tengoku* [Paradise on Earth] continued to be published by the church headquarters after Mr. Okada's death, but the list below covers only the period through June 1954, when his original articles ceased appearing in them.

BIBLIOGRAPHY

I. Books

1. *Myōnichi no ijutsu* [Medicine for Tomorrow], 3 vols. (Tokyo: Takeshi Shiozawa, 1942–43), 951 pp. + xx.
2. *Tengoku no fukuin* [The Gospels of Heaven] (Tokyo: Katsuyuki Sakai, 1947), 409 pp. + xiv.
3. *Shinkō zatsuwa* [Essays on Faith] (Tokyo: Nihon Kannon Kyōdan, 1949), 106 pp. + vi.
4. *Reikai sōdan* [Glimpses into the Spiritual World] (Atami, Shizuoka pref.: Nijusseiki Shuppan Insatsu Gōshigaisha, 1949), 77 pp.
5. *Jikan zuidan* [Assorted Reflections] (Atami: Nijusseiki Shuppan Insatsu Gōshigaisha, 1949), 76 pp.
6. *Kiseki monogatari* [Stories of Miracles] (Atami: Nijusseiki Shuppan Insatsu Gōshigaisha, 1949), 78 pp.
7. *Akemaro kin'eishū* [Selected Poems of Akemaro] (Odawara, Kanagawa pref.: Nihon Miroku Kyōkai, 1949), 86 pp.
8. *Hikari e no michi* [The Pathway to Light] (Odawara: Nihon Miroku Kyōkai, 1949), 69 pp.
9. *Yama to mizu* [Mountain and Stream] (Tokyo: Kaichirō Kosaka, 1950), 301 pp. + viii.
10. *Shinji no kenkōhō* [A Divinely-inspired Approach to Health] (Tokyo: Kyūsei Shimbunsha, 1950), 72 pp.
11. *Sekai Meshiyakyō hayawakari* [An Introduction to Sekai Meshiyakyō] (Tokyo: Eikōsha, 1950), 57 pp.
12. *Shizen nōhō kaisetsu* [Notes on Nature Farming] (Tokyo: Eikōsha, 1951), 63 pp.; revised and enlarged edition (Atami: Sekai Meshiyakyō Shuppanbu, 1953), 236 pp. + viii.
13. *Sanka-shū* [Collected Hymns] (Atami: Sekai Meshiyakyō Shuppanbu, 1951), 107 pp. + iv.
14. *Kekkaku shinkō ryōhō* [Spiritual Healing of Tuberculosis] (Atami: Sekai Meshiyakyō Shuppanbu, 1952), 235 pp. + iv.
15. *Sekai Meshiyakyō kiseki-shū* [God Works Miracles] (Atami: Sekai Meshiyakyō Shuppanbu, 1953), 300 pp. + xi; revised edition (1954), 302 pp. + xi.
16. Sekai Meshiyakyō Kyōmubu, ed., *Goshinsho: Shūkyō-hen* [Essays

on Religion] (Atami: Sekai Meshiyakyō Shuppanbu, 1954), 520 pp. + x.

17. ———, ed., *Sekai Meshiyakyō seiten: Geijutsu-hen, shakai-hen* [Essays on Art and Society] (Atami: Sekai Meshiyakyō Shuppanbu, 1955), 318 pp. + vii.

II. Transcriptions

18. Shinsei Kyōkai, ed., *Gokōwa-roku* [Record of Enlightening Talks], vols. 1–19 (Tokyo: Shinsei Kyōkai, 1948–50).
19. Sekai Meshiyakyō Henshūbu, ed., *Gosuiji-roku* [Record of Instructions], vols. 1–30 (Atami: Sekai Meshiyakyō Shuppanbu, 1951–54).
20. ———, ed., *Mioshie-shū* [Record of Oral Teachings], vols. 1–33 (Atami: Sekai Meshiyakyō Shuppanbu, 1951–54).

III. Pastoral Aids Compiled by Disciples

21. Ichiro Nakamura, ed., *Dendō no tebiki* [Guide to Ministry] (Osaka: Daijō Kyōkai, 1954), 178 pp. + xiii; revised fifth edition (Kyoto: Seikō Kyōkai, 1959), 316 pp. + xxvii.
22. ———, ed., *Johrei* [Johrei] (Kobe: Kikō Kyōkai, 1955), 83 pp. + x; revised second edition (Kyoto: Seikō Kyōkai, 1957), 85 pp. + ix.
23. ———, ed., *Goyō ni tsuite* [Sacred Service] (Kobe: Kikō Kyōkai, 1955); revised fourth edition (Kyoto: Seikō Kyōkai, 1959), 108 pp. + vi.
24. ———, ed., *Nyūshin* [Belief] (Kobe: Kikō Kyōkai, 1956), 87 pp. + vi.
25. ———, ed., *Johrei fukyō* [Ministry of Healing] (Kobe: Kikō Kyōkai, 1956), 80 pp. + iii; enlarged second edition (Kyoto: Seikō Kyōkai, 1958), 118 pp. + iv.
26. ———, ed., *Tsumi ni tsuite* [Sin] (Kyoto: Seikō Kyōkai), 186 pp. + xiii.
27. ———, ed., *Sōnen* [On Ideas] (Kyoto: Seikō Kyōkai, 1957), 97 pp. + v.

IV. Periodicals

28. *Hikari* [Light], nos. 1–47, March 8, 1949–January 28, 1950. Edited by Kaichirō Kosaka and published in Tokyo, first by Nihon Kannon Kyōdan and later by Nihon Miroku Kyōkai.
29. *Kyūsei* [Salvation], nos. 48–65, February 4, 1950–June 3, 1950. Edited by Kaichirō Kosaka and published in Tokyo by Hikarisha.
30. *Eikō* [Glory], nos. 66–258, August 23, 1950–May 26, 1954. Nos. 66–115 edited by Masao Koyama, nos. 116–149 by Umeno Koyama, and nos. 150–258 by Seiichi Momomi. Nos. 66–149 published in Tokyo by Eikōsha and nos. 150–258 by Sekai Meshiyakyō Shuppanbu in Atami.
31. *Chijō tengoku* [Paradise on Earth], nos. 1–59, December 1948–June 1954. Edited by Jitsutarō Moriyama and published in Atami by Sekai Meshiyakyō Shuppanbu since 1950.

Commentary on Basic Concepts

CREATION   The act of God by which, as part of His plan, He makes everything in the universe.

THE pillar of Mr. Okada's teaching is his doctrine on creation, whose premise is that everything in the universe is made by God in accordance with the eternal divine plan. God created man last and gave him a spiritual nature, with a soul capable of understanding His will as He makes it known to people. God allows man to attain the knowledge and skill necessary to govern other creatures.

God's creation is purposive; it is directed towards preparing humankind for earthly paradise. By carrying out the divinely appointed task of building a world of goodness, truth, and beauty, man prepares for the new civilization. For that reason, each person is born with a specific mission, whose fulfillment represents his individual contribution. Thus everyone is equipped with his own physical, intellectual, emotional, and other characteristics to help him carry out his mission.

All the other creatures were made to support man in fulfilling the task God gave him. God also created beauty and variety in nature, the seasons, and the different climates, to be pleasing to man. While God filled the world with His glory in snow-capped mountains, emerald seas, brilliant leaves and flowers, He also gave to each environment, each separate plant, animal, mineral and all else in nature, a specific role in the totality of His plan. Even the lowliest grasses and the most undistinguished rocks have some part to play. To use something for a purpose He did not assign to it is to violate the spiritual laws of creation. Man, for his part, if he turns to God for help and lives with the certainty of knowing that God will respond, can live in harmony with Him. Man has the capacity to recognize that his only support is God's infinite love and to love God as he is loved by Him.

The universe God created consists of spiritual and material realms. He presides over it all through His governance of the spiritual world, but He also directly intervenes in the realm of matter. The human soul, while it is enclosed within the body, actually belongs to the realm of spirit. When a person dies, his soul leaves the body and remains fully in the spiritual world.

God ordained the universe to be governed by laws, one of the most important being the law of spiritual dominance over the material. Purification, also, is a basic principle in the life of man and nature. God determined the order of things in the universe and He laid out a schedule according to which His plan for this world is realized. Man is given the highest status among all mortal creatures, but at the same time he is bound to abide by a set of commandments. The other creatures, animate or inanimate, spontaneously perform their own functions with the inborn abilities God gave each of them.

Mr. Okada stressed that because living creatures, particularly man, are made and sustained by God, they are capable of performing in ways that cannot be explained by scientific knowledge or rational analysis. Precisely because God created man to be responsible for the fulfillment of His plan on earth, human birth and death are directly under His control. When a person's mission in the world has come to an end, no human power can prolong his life. Nor must any but God's power end a life before its mission is completed. That is why God gave us the knowledge of Johrei—in that gift He has provided a creative force to help us overcome our physical and spiritual imperfections and carry out our mission to its completion.

When man decided to go his own way instead of God's, in defiance of the very purpose of divine creation, he sinned, and human life became filled with misery. In His love God wants to forgive man, and He continues to wait until people repent. God wills that everyone be awakened to knowledge of His existence. He ordains that sin and unhappiness themselves become a catalyst to encourage man finally to accept His love, and understanding His purpose for creation, to participate in the building of earthly paradise.

God loves all people and wants to help those who repent. As a person's soul is cleansed and he returns to God's path, his thoughts, words, and actions become pure and good. He is no longer in rebellion against God; he lives his faith every moment of his life, and at last he experiences a personal love for God that fully reciprocates God's love for him. He reaches a point where his love for other people becomes full and true. This is earthly paradise, the imminent goal of creation. It is an ideal state of man and nature that represents the perfection of God's plan for this world.

Beauty, harmony, and all the wonders of creation that will blossom in Paradise on Earth are but means or conditions for the fulfillment of a more profound goal. All of God's acts, including His forgiveness of our sins, are directed towards that goal, which is the salvation of mankind. Earthly paradise is to be built by those people whom God judges can be saved, and it is to be inhabited by those who attain a level of spiritual awakening whereby they follow God's will for them in its totality. Those so truly blessed will have eternal life through their union with the divine and shall see God in heaven. This is the ultimate goal of creation.

FAITH Commitment to a personal relationship with God based on love for Him; trust and confidence in God's existence and His will to save man.

Faith is a promise and it stems from a kind of knowledge we can attain only by grace. It is not something we can pick up or throw away anytime at our discretion. Nor can it be imposed on someone from without. Faith is genuine only when it springs forth, by God's grace, from within the depth of one's soul. For these reasons, Mr. Okada emphasized the importance of letting one's love for God grow spontaneously in the development of individual faith.

Mr. Okada had to overcome deep-rooted traditions of polytheism as he worked to spread his teachings in Japan. The vast majority of his followers had no notion of God, the one Lord and Creator, and it was extremely difficult to convince them of the reality of God's presence. Mr. Okada's ministry of healing was primarily a means to help guide unbelievers, as well as Buddhists and Shintoists, to accept the love of God through the saving light of Johrei.

Belief in God's existence is only the starting point in the process of conversion to faith. "Anyone who has witnessed God's work in the extraordinary blessings of Johrei ought to strive to deepen his faith," Mr. Okada taught. "He is a God of love who wants to save as many people as possible. The best way to respond to His love is to help those in distress, to give them Johrei and lead them to faith in God." Thus, Mr. Okada encouraged his followers to engage actively in the service of healing so that they could develop their faith through committed outreach to others.

Mr. Okada also stressed that we must entrust everything to God if we wish to deepen our faith. "The divine light of Johrei, by which many have been saved from certain death, is evidence of God's absolute goodness and omnipotence. Have complete confidence in that," he said. The healing power of Johrei is God's gift to man. It cleanses the spiritual and physical body systems, removing the sources of our afflictions. But Johrei often does more than just heal sickness. It can awaken a person to the truth of God through his experience of the miraculous nature of that power, and if he tries to live his new-found faith as best as he can, his soul will begin to be purified. By leaving everything to divine grace and accepting even pain and suffering as God's will, he will be able to develop genuine faith.

Mr. Okada said that an essential qualification for Johrei administrators is complete trust and strong faith in God. Whenever a disciple faced difficulties in his healing ministry, the founder invariably discovered that his faith was weak or weakening. "Inadequate faith shows itself in lack of zeal in regular worship at the church, reading the teaching, or even in negligence of one's duties."

The need for repentance is the core of Mr. Okada's teaching, but he rarely dwelt on that explicitly, either in sermons or counseling. He deliberately waited for his followers to develop a faith mature enough to let them repent of their own volition. Rather than directly censuring an act of wrongdoing, Mr. Okada preferred to guide the person step by step towards repentance. With those whose faith was sure and firm, however, Mr. Okada was very strict and spared no time reprimanding them for their sins. He spoke of various levels of penitence, but he laid particular emphasis on the need to be wary of and to overcome any thought lurking in one's heart that contravenes God's will.

A person of genuine faith tries to follow God's will in everything he does. His ultimate goal is to become a perfect person through complete obedience to God's commands. To that end, Mr. Okada taught, the faithful must constantly seek God's grace for the purification of the soul and strive to be absolutely pure and honest in thought, word, and deed.

The more one reads Mr. Okada's writings, based on God's revelation to him, the purer his soul becomes, and the deeper his faith. Whereas channeling Johrei cleanses the spirit from without, reading God's words in the scriptures generates purificatory power from within. Similarly, offering prayers to God elevates the spirit of the supplicant and deepens his faith.

Faith is essentially an individual matter, but Mr. Okada recognized the crucial part the church organization also plays in the growth of faith. Because the divine spirit works through the agency of the church, it is important for the faithful to attend services. Along with Johrei and Mr. Okada's teaching, the church performs a valuable role in guiding believers towards genuine, pure faith. The church is not only the nucleus of proselytizing activities, but the interpreter of the messages God sends to man by way of miracles and other acts in the world.

It is not difficult to discern an element of eschatology in Mr. Okada's thought. The revelation he received focuses on the imminence of the judgment and the hope of salvation in earthly paradise. The gift of Johrei is a sign of God's forgiveness. Yet belief in God and the practice of Johrei alone are not enough to assure that one will survive the judgment. Each believer must truly repent and return to God's path; those whose faith remains superficial and insincere will be subjected to intensive purification as the time of judgment draws near, urging them, too, to repent.

Already changes have begun in the realm of spirit, where the purificatory power is now steadily growing stronger. And we are beginning to see the repercussions of that spiritual transformation in the realm of matter. The rise of many complex, often terminal disease syndromes is one of the signs all around us that herald the forthcoming upheaval. Mr. Okada warns that if people continue to profess only a faltering faith, despite the enormous blessings they have received through Johrei, eventually they will have to pay for their lack of gratitude. If they repent as they reap what they have sown, they will be given a chance of returning to God's path; otherwise they will be doomed. Rather than vainly trying to help ungrateful people, it is more important, Mr. Okada said, to spread the knowledge of Johrei to as many multitudes as possible throughout the world, reaching those who have yet to profess faith in God, the Creator.

GOD   The one ultimate, supreme Being. Creator and
Lord of the universe.

In his teaching on God, Mr. Okada tended to emphasize five aspects in particular: the oneness of God
as Creator and Lord of the universe; the presence of
God everywhere in the universe and throughout nature,
history, society, and daily life; God as love that extends
to all his creatures, especially man; God as the ultimate
spiritual existence; and His work as it relates to human
spiritual and physical health. He expressed the reality
of God using such words as "almighty," "omniscient,"
"absolute," "eternal," "perfect," and "infinite."

Mr. Okada's teachings concerning the nature of God
and faith in Him have not yet been thoroughly cate-
gorized or analyzed, and in reading them, one must
always be aware of the broad conceptual framework
in which he placed them. It is clear that all of Mr.
Okada's teaching on God is based on the revelations
he received in 1926 and later, and on the inspirations he experienced in his communion with God during
his thirty years of active ministry. He is recorded as
saying, "God tells me of His plans whenever He deems
it necessary," and "I am nothing more than an instrument for God." But he never completed the work of preparing a systematic exposition of the messages and their
implications.

Mr. Okada tried to relay to his followers the divine
messages he received by pointing to miraculous events

that took place in the course of his ministry. God has a grand design for the salvation of humankind, Mr. Okada taught. He is steadily carrying out His plan for this world, and each miracle that occurs is a visible sign of His grace and a concrete manifestation that the divine task is advancing towards completion.

God is often referred to as "Creator" or "Lord" in Mr. Okada's writing. References to Him as the fount of love and mercy appear just as frequently, but that aspect of God's nature is described most explicitly in teachings on divine blessings, in which God's love is usually explained in terms of the miracles He performs to save man. Every time the light of Johrei brought about miraculous healing, Mr. Okada made a point of stressing the unfathomable greatness of God's love and power.

God is not someone "up there" far out of the reach of man. "God is right here with us all the time, watching over His children with boundless love and warmth," Mr. Okada taught. On the basis of his personal experience, he advised us to "leave everything to God and live always under His omniscient care." If we do, we, too, can find a life of peace and supreme human fulfillment.

Mr. Okada dwelt long upon the profundity of God's love and the abundance of His blessings, but he also made it clear how relentless God can be towards those who stubbornly refuse to repent. Whenever a disciple knowingly committed a sin or misguided other church members through some kind of devious behavior, the founder would admonish him: "It is no use apologizing to me. Pray to God and beg His forgiveness, and do so from the bottom of your heart."

God's presence in the midst of our lives makes Him real to anyone who acknowledges Him, but the awareness of God's presence does not by itself guarantee that we are really capable of understanding God's special wishes for each of us. "God's will is unfathomable. Without help from Him, it is simply beyond human wisdom and intelligence. Only he who knows how little he understands God, knows something about God." Abandon all arrogance and listen to the voice of God with absolute obedience and humility, then you will be a person of faith, Mr. Okada taught, and you can sense with increasing accuracy what it is God wishes you to do.

MAN   The highest among the mortal creatures; the only one with the ability to differentiate between good and evil, and the only one having the potential for understanding the divine will.

God gave man a spiritual nature deep enough that he could, if he truly desired, understand His will, and He also gave man intelligence to reign justly over all other creatures. By virtue of the inherent spiritual power of moral discernment and strength of will that God gave him, man can distinguish between good and evil. Those qualities are necessary to allow positive participation in fulfilling God's plan for this world. But God also granted man freedom in what to think, which always gives him a choice of following good or evil in his thoughts, words, and behavior. Thus man has the potential to attain a state of saintliness, while he can also betray God's love and degrade himself to the depths of animality.

For man, freedom and responsibility are like two sides of the same coin. One cannot exercise freedom without being responsible for the consequences. The decision to follow good or evil is a responsibility that ultimately resides in the soul.

The soul is created to receive God's will for each person, but when man turned from God's path, his soul lost its original purity. With his fall from grace, moreover, man began to commit sins, and as a result his understanding of the divine will was obscured. His proclivity towards evil grew stronger; his soul became increasingly beclouded as he continued to sin and he was alienated further from God.

All humans are equal before God, but the mission each individual is assigned by Him differs. The individual mission represents the way God wishes the person to work in this world, but it also reflects the purity of his soul. The purer the soul and the more strongly inclined towards good, the higher its rank will be on the spiritual ladder, and the more noble its mission. One's ability, character and other personal attributes, also, correspond with the nature of the particular mission he has received from God. Man also has desires, which help him maintain life and propagate it, and which enable him to enjoy the many divine blessings of this world—the beauty of nature, works of art, pleasure in daily life and work.

With all these and more is man's nature endowed; they are ordinary gifts freely given by God. Yet, man would receive blessings in even greater abundance if he were earnest in his mission and faithful to God. If, however, the soul is not pure enough to control the desires, they can grow overbearingly strong and lead a person to sin. Sin, an act that counters God's will, is a primary source of unhappiness. Anyone, nonetheless, even those in the worst misery, can begin a new, happy life if they will accept God's grace and steadily purify their souls, living the will of God through faith and through works dedicated to Him.

> He who goes forth
> to embrace
> the great love of God
> is truly human.
>
> (Mokichi Okada, April 1949)

MIRACLES   Those works that can only be wrought by almighty power and that God chooses to perform directly in the world of His creatures.

Mr. Okada explained miracles as the wondrous or extraordinary occurrences that take place in the experience of people whose lives are devoted to healing through Johrei. There is no completely rational way to explain miracles or the impact they have. Although the people who have experienced miracles cannot describe them scientifically, their testimony remains the most potent, articulate, and impressive source of information about the character and force of miracles.

From Mr. Okada's teaching and the long, varied experience of his followers, we know that miracles 1) serve as a means for God to announce His presence to man and to make man aware of the reality of His existence; 2) are a declaration of God's love for man and attest to the great power of the Creator; and 3) are an announcement from God that He wishes to help man repent, and that He will forgive and save all those who repent of their sins.

Miracles are one of God's ways of guiding human hearts in the direction of good and leading as many souls as possible to repentance. When people receive Johrei and experience God's healing power firsthand, they are invariably struck with awe. They are inspired to recognize the blessings that come from faith in God, and often this experience starts them firmly on the path to conversion. The incredible event of a great healing miracle of Johrei also deepens the faith of those who witness it, including those who channeled the divine light at the time.

No one but God can decide when or if a miracle will occur. When a person feels strong hatred or jealousy, is obsessed, or has some other immoderate or evil sensations; or when God wishes someone to understand the harmful influence of his evil acts and to repent, miracles may fail to occur for him. Sometimes even the most devoted, unselfish people find that when they have deviated just a little from God's path in something they thought, said, or did, miracles no longer happen. With the help of Mr. Okada's teaching, however, they are guided to the heart of faith and gradually understand its true purpose, which is to live in as close conformity as possible with God's will, and to strive for genuine repentance.

PROVIDENCE God's work in guiding man along His path to salvation, and God's plan to have man build a world of truth, goodness, and beauty on earth in perfect accord with His will.

Mr. Okada's teaching on providence centers on the relationship of God, Creator and arbiter of all things, to man. Our world is deluged with evil and suffering because man has not carried out the divine will; instead, he turned against God and brought on himself an ever growing tendency to sin. But providence is also divine forbearance—God's patient and loving encouragement of man to return to His path. The messages that He has transmitted by way of revelations to the faithful through the ages tell all people to repent and receive His forgiveness.

Further, we know that God's providence is dynamic. The divine will on earth often is made known and realized through the instrumentality of material civilization, which is also to be the tool for man when he fashions a good and beautiful world. Despite their many negative consequences, scientific progress and technological development make the physical aspects of human existence easier, and they free people from certain labors to enable them to pursue cultural, religious, or charitable activities.

Few people have honestly tried to fathom their wrongdoing and errors, but even so, God's infinite love for man has never abated. Now, Mr. Okada said, at a time when man is so widely separated from God, we can go no further on the road of evil; we can continue our aimless wandering from Him no longer. As His providence brings us closer to the judgment, we need to live with the hope of God's forgiveness of the repentant. He revealed Johrei to Mr. Okada as a visible sign which would help lead us to faith and repentance.

Mr. Okada preached that God's judgment is imminent, and he pointed out the many other signs He has given through the great religious teachings, miracles, and His works in the world. Those who respond to God's call to repent must be judged and cleansed of evil. Then they will be prepared to obey God's will in the building of earthly paradise.

REVELATION The transmission of God's word and His truth to man, both directly and through divine messengers, and the manifestation of His will in human history.

Mr. Okada taught that history is the manifestation of God's will, that God reveals Himself in the context of human history. Divine revelations have come to certain people at different times, in different regions and cultures, transmitted to show them the road to salvation. Most of the world religions are based on such historic revelations.

God's first revelation to Mr. Okada, which occurred towards the end of 1926, marks his awakening to the mission God gave him in the world (see A Brief Biography). He learned that the time was drawing near for God's judgment and the end of evil, and that people must repent and ask for forgiveness for their wrongdoing. Central to all of the revelations Mr. Okada received at that time was the declaration by God that earthly paradise was approaching, to be built by those whose sins have been forgiven. God commanded Mr. Okada to convey the news to people throughout the world.

Japan has no tradition of monotheistic religion. God, the one Lord and Creator of all things, is an alien concept to most Japanese. Moreover, there is a very strong tendency towards unbelief among intellectuals. Thus, the significance of God's revelation to Mr. Okada must be understood, first of all, in the context of Japan's peculiar religious climate.

Our mentor's mission involved much more than informing his countrymen of God's salvation. He was called on to bring the message to all the faithful in the world as well as to those who, distracted by the development of materialistic civilization and the progress of science and technology, find themselves alienated from genuine faith. Mr. Okada made special efforts to appeal to those lost in the complexity of modern civilization, encouraging them to let the power of Johrei awaken their souls and let his teaching guide their faith towards true love for God.

The truth of Johrei was revealed as a concrete sign that God wants man to build a new world. Through the knowledge and practice of Johrei, hundreds of thousands of people have embraced faith in Him. Mr. Okada told his followers that his divinely-inspired teaching would enable each person to discern the voice of God amidst the cacophony of messages that confound our hearts and minds.

Mr. Okada also explained that the construction of earthly paradise is "a joint project of God and man." People will participate in the project as workers to build a new world according to God's design. Mr. Okada saw himself as a foreman or supervising engineer—which makes his teaching a kind of blueprint illustrating the guidelines and specifications for the task.

God's revelations to Mr. Okada occurred in several different ways. Sometimes an event or accident took place to reveal God's will in a manner of prefiguration. At other times, divine wisdom was relayed to Mr. Okada by the spirit of a messenger from God. He also said that he heard divine voices from within. In his later years when he attained a high level of spiritual enlightenment, he often knew God's will almost intuitively. However they occurred, each revelation was followed by miracles or sudden progress in his mission, bearing out the truth and validity of the revelation.

In running his church, Mr. Okada relied on "guidance from God" for his major decisions. "At those times God instructed me with just a word or two." After the war, when the church organization had been firmly established and Mr. Okada himself moved into the final phase of his mission on earth, he underwent a personal transformation. That finally enabled him to overcome the separation from God that had been a universal element in the human condition until then. Before he died, his thoughts in meditation were one with God's will.

SIN Any thought, word, or action by which a person knowingly and willingly violates or opposes the will of God.

Mr. Okada's concept of sin, for the most part, is similar to ideas of wrong and sin as understood in the foremost Oriental and Judeo-Christian traditions. He explained sin as being, first and foremost, rebellion by man against God; it is man's refusal to accept God's love and to heed the divine call for repentance. By extension, sin is also an offense against the self and fellow humans.

Although sin originates in the heart of the individual, the soul is ultimately responsible for all sinful thoughts, words, and acts. Mr. Okada explained this as follows: man's disobedience to God is the original source of clouds on the soul, which is the locus of will and intellect and is the free decision-making agent in man. Clouds weaken the powers of will and intellect and thereby undermine the soul's capacity to receive God's messages and withstand evil. When the soul is clouded, it cannot freely control the activities of the elemental spirit and cannot always prevent inordinate desires from swaying the heart. Nor can a clouded soul effectively resist the evil influences of an alien spirit that may enter the heart. As a person continues to sin, the clouds on his soul increase and so does the misery he both experiences and generates.

Sin is thus inward and individual, but its manifestations are more often than not outward and social. Along with malice, greed, jealousy, deceit, conceit, and laziness, Mr. Okada condemned theft, adultery, violence, murder, abortion, exploitation of others, and all forms of personal and social injustice as acts against God and man. He was especially adamant in his denunciation of homicide and suicide, as well as any acts that inflict injury or damage on human lives, including one's own. While stressing the inherently individual nature of sin, Mr. Okada also pointed out that an entire group can collectively commit sins when the souls of its members are clouded. Thus, a community or even a nation is just as capable of sinning as an individual. War is a prime example of collective sin.

Mr. Okada advised his disciples that God judges every sin separately, and each involves different motivations, acts, consequences, and so on. Basically, he said, the gravity of sin is commensurate with the sinner's awareness of how far his action conflicts with the divine will. Depending on the level of that awareness, an evil act can become proportionately graver. The deeper one's faith, the more serious any act of deviation from God's path. Similarly, the more important one's mission, the greater his responsibility to prevent evil thoughts, words, or deeds in himself.

Both the motivation and result of an act must be considered in evaluating the seriousness of sin. Mr. Okada distinguished sins from morally evil acts committed unintentionally, out of ignorance, or out of misapprehension of evil for good. Sins—evil acts committed out of evil intentions—are by far the most harmful. But even if the motivation is good, acts whose consequences bring misery or harm to others or oneself are very serious. Deliberately distorting the truth, or rationalizing an idea or action that contravenes the truth, Mr. Okada said, are among the most ignoble sins. Propagation of prejudiced, atheistic, or other misconceived doctrines is also a grave sin. A fanatic movement to spread beliefs that run counter to the will of God can lead to oppression, or at worst, the annihilation of millions.

One specific type of sin Mr. Okada emphasized is conceit. Followers who administer Johrei and channel the light that cures the sick sometimes forget that the real source of the healing power is God. They unconsciously commit the sin of blasphemy by mistaking divine power for their own, or by misleading others in arbitrary interpretations of God's will. To assume that the small mind of a human being can comprehend the whole of God's will, and failing that, end up obstructing it, is a serious sin. To fully understand God is not possible for man; nor were human beings made to be able to judge all that is good or evil or to pass judgment on other people. Unless we are always conscious of God in our lives, it is all too easy to commit terrible sins without knowing what we are doing. Mr. Okada cautions us to recognize the limits of our own powers of judgment and to build faith so that we approach life with the humility of the knowledge that God *is* our life, on whom we rely for everything.

Mr. Okada sometimes said, "No matter how grave a sin, God will always forgive the sinner if his repentance is genuine and thorough. On the other hand, no matter how trifling the sin, God will always punish the sinner if he does not repent." Sincere repentance is to seek forgiveness and to ask God for absolution. Also, through the agency of the soul, God helps man to refrain from sinning. Our conscience hurts when we harbor evil thoughts or commit sinful acts, for example. When self-love is too strong for a person to hear the voice of conscience, it brings harm to himself and society and much unhappiness.

God freely gives grace to anyone who genuinely tries to abide by His will and live as a tool for Him. There are certain deeds that virtually always represent a sincere, selfless response to God's love. To save the life of another person by transmitting the divine light of Johrei to him; to bring the news of

God's salvation to sceptics and agnostics and guide them into sincere faith; or to pray for the peace of souls now in the spiritual world—these are all examples of highly commendable deeds.

When his followers came for help in times of trouble or affliction, to some Mr. Okada emphasized the sin that all people carry because they are human, and to others he stressed the purifying aspect of suffering or the ease with which they could overcome difficulties if they relied totally on God. To still others he stressed the command to repent and try to live a better, more charitable life. In all his counsel, Mr. Okada pointed out the need for repentance, because those who truly repent, he said, will be given the power to overcome the evil in themselves.

Yet when they try to repent, many find that the deeper their understanding of the faith, the more profoundly they feel the enormity of their sin and realize how difficult it is to overcome it. Man's turning away from God is a sin that an individual can fathom only with great effort as he tries to overcome the tendency to sin in his everyday life. Mr. Okada nevertheless encouraged a sense of individual responsibility towards God by constantly warning believers to work hard to become better people themselves and not to judge others. "Only God knows whether a person is really good or evil in his heart," he said. In other words, God alone can tell whether one has truly repented or not.

WISDOM God's gift to man of the spiritual power to grasp and respond to divine messages; the working of the soul to deepen one's faith and moral knowledge.

From the various ways Mr. Okada used the term wisdom in his talks and writing, it is possible to identify two basic levels of meaning: religious, and moral or practical. On the deepest, religious level, wisdom refers to the purity and responsiveness of the soul to God. Mr. Okada explained wisdom primarily as the extraordinary capacity, determined by the purity of the soul, that enables a person to understand and commit himself to the truths made known to him by divine grace. God wishes to save us from misery and forgive our sins so that we may build a new world of absolute goodness where His will is to be fully realized. God sends messages to the soul whenever He deems it necessary to help someone carry out his particular mission in the fulfillment of the divine plan. It is wisdom that tells a person what those messages mean and how to respond.

Because the souls of most people are so clouded by sin, however, they are not always responsive. "The Lord tells us many different things, depending on time, place, and the degree of our spiritual purity," Mr. Okada said. If we repent of our sins and are forgiven, the clouds will decrease and we will grow in spiritual purity and, therefore, in wisdom. When Mr. Okada said, "Refine your wisdom, and you will hear God," he meant that we must pray for forgiveness and the perception to let us recognize God's word. He advised his followers always to pray and, if they could not grasp the message immediately, to wait until they understood what God was telling them.

Wisdom is not acquired; it is granted by God to those who believe and try to hear Him and improve their lives. Wisdom helps one to see deep inside himself and to know how to live in goodness and happiness. One with wisdom can guide others, for he or she is assured of access to God's truths. Love is an essential part of wisdom, and with greater wisdom one grows in the love of God and fellow humans. Wisdom also lets one distinguish between self-centered concerns and those that genuinely express love. A person of wisdom, therefore, is not only always responsive to the will of God, but also has a deep insight into the minds of the people he tries to help.

Thus Mr. Okada emphasized the importance of wisdom in pastoral work—guiding people into sincere faith and true happiness. As transmitters of God's will, pastors must have love and wisdom, as well as zeal to help those in need. Mr. Okada urged his disciples constantly to seek purification of their souls and deeper wisdom.

Because a person of wisdom willingly gives himself over to God to become a tool in the realization of the divine plan, the mission he is given by God is always an important one. This kind of person can accept the mystery of God's revelation to Mr. Okada, and the teaching based on it. As summed up in the "Prayer of

Johrei," the essence of the teaching is the certainty of salvation for all those whose penitence is genuine. In that sense, wisdom means the awareness and repentance of our betrayal of God's love through the ages and the assurance that sincere faith in Him will bring us His forgiveness.

On another level, Mr. Okada spoke of wisdom in practical terms of behavior and moral conduct. For example, he repeatedly stressed timing in counsel as crucial to effective pastoral work. Using the metaphor of a falling stone, he said, "Don't try to stop it while it is rolling down the slope. Let it go until it lands at a level spot midway, or even until it reaches the bottom. A truly wise person knows exactly when and where to retrieve the stone." In other words, it is not necessarily wise to reprimand or advise someone regarding some unkind, evil, or damaging deed when the perpetrator is still engrossed in his activity. He may be still unaware of how it hurts others or how much he will regret it later. If you upbraid him prematurely, it will only cause a reaction and he may go too far, until he reaches a point of no return. It will be much better if the sinner becomes aware of his wrongdoing himself, for then his repentance will be true, generated from within. Wisdom tells you when and how such a person can best be helped.

Mr. Okada also admonished his disciples "not to try to be too wise." "Just do the job you have been given by God. Do it as well as you can, and leave the rest up to Him," he taught. By that, he meant that a truly wise person does his best to perform his assignments with prudence and objectivity, and waits for God's assessment of the results. The person who has overcome self-righteousness and self-centeredness, and knows how little he knows, does not go by his own standards, but by God's. "If a sick person comes to you for help," Mr. Okada said in making this point, "just do the best you can to take care of him. Do not anticipate the results—what will happen if you succeed in healing him, for example."

By the same logic, Mr. Okada warned against trying to impose the wish to help on anyone who shuns Johrei, even if that person is influential or outstanding in some way. "Do not think in terms of what good it would do if you persuaded someone to join the church. It may be a human approach, but not God's." That was one way of telling his followers not to pass judgment on people on the basis of sex or race, appearance, education, fame, wealth, or any other superficial attributes. Speaking of proselytizing activities, Mr. Okada said, "Do not exclude certain types of people simply because of their social reputation." Anyone who so desires should be allowed to join the church, he taught. "It is God's decision, not ours, whether a person joins or not."

Appendices

I. Clinical Study With Johrei

FOR people today, whose attitudes and patterns of thought have been molded by the demands of logic inherent in our scientific and rationalistic society, it is often extremely difficult, if not impossible, to accept a phenomenon on faith alone. They may find in it an instinctual appeal, or their own hopes, needs, or suffering may open their hearts to it as they seek fulfillment, but their minds too often reject it if it cannot be proved. This is only human, for our responses are geared to our training and experience, and not many of us today are trained to accept what has not in some way been verified scientifically.

A Unique Project

To those who have experienced the effects of Johrei, there is no need for further proof that it does indeed convey the power to heal. It is not possible to offer proof that this is divine power; the acceptance of that is an individual matter. But Johrei as a healing agent has been verified time and again through improvement in and recovery from disease, physical injury, and spiritual afflictions. Still, among those who have not had this experience, it is rare to find people who will accept it, even tentatively, as a possible answer to their afflictions in the same way that they accept medical science.

The practitioners and recipients of Johrei know it to be an effective method of healing that is neither risky nor damaging. For people unfamiliar with it, however, neither our church's convictions nor even demonstrations of them are usually enough to present a persuasive case for the power to heal of Johrei, which, precisely because it seems to flout all the known laws of science, appears inconceivable. That is why it was decided to set up a formal clinical study introducing Johrei in a controlled environment where the results could be scientifically recorded.

For a period of eleven months, from January through November 1981, Teruyuki Tada of the Reimei Church in Kyoto helped to conduct a unique study at one of the leading cancer research centers in the United States. It was called "The Effects of Johrei on Patients with Terminal Lung Cancer." At the beginning, the word "psychosomatic healing" was used instead of "Johrei," mainly for the benefit of the participants at the institute who were not familiar with the Japanese word, but since "psychosomatic healing" is not an entirely accurate description, the term was changed.

For the study, the Japanese collaborator administered Johrei to cancer patients, and doctors and staff gathered data and evaluated the results. There were several objectives. Broadly, they were (1) to test the purely physical response of patients to Johrei, and (2) to test the psychophysical, or subjective, response. It was originally planned to test the specific physical response by monitoring the size and number of tumor masses for changes, but these tests were not made. It was decided to test the subjective response by observing changes in performance status as indexed by the Karnofsky scale; recording the type and amount of analgesics, hypnotics, and sedatives used; and administering the McGill pain questionnaire to detect changes in amount and type of pain experienced. In other words, use of these established methods was intended to provide statistical data concerning physical changes in the illness, including side-effects, changes in the patients' sense of comfort, pain, and their general attitude, and finally, if possible, the extent to which conventional treatment hinders the work of Johrei.

Method and Participants

The basic method was to randomize 32 patients to a two-arm (treated vs. control) study. Those eligible for the experiment were patients with advanced (inoperable) lung cancer who did not respond to or relapsed after a course of chemotherapy and/or radiation therapy. Conventional treatment could offer only transient palliative measures. Their median survival was estimated at three to four months. Rev. Tada administered Johrei to those in the treated experimental group whenever feasible at the discretion of the physician, who was responsible for the clinical study. This treatment was administered in conjunction with conventional medical treatment in each case.

Patient response was evaluated by length of survival after randomization and through a series of interviews based on a questionnaire. The questionnaire incorporated a "vitagram" scale assessing general quality of life based on physical status, a modified McGill pain questionnaire, and a quality of life questionnaire regarding nausea, mood, appetite, fatigue, concentration, personal appearance, and pain.

All the interviews were conducted by one of two people. An initial interview was held at the time of randomization, with follow-up interviews conducted as often as possible at intervals of at least two weeks. Twelve of the patients from the total of 32 completed only one interview, providing no evaluable information, and so these twelve, and two others who were too incapacitated to complete a significant proportion of any follow-up questionnaire, were omitted from analysis. In the end, data provided by 18 patients, 9 treated and 9 control, were used for analysis.

Including those whose data could not, finally, be analyzed, the collaborator administered Johrei to 20 patients in a total of 373 sessions, the greater part of which were conducted between January and June. Obviously the number of sessions with each patient varied widely. One female patient did not return to the hospital after the first session. One male patient received Johrei only twice. The other 18 patients received Johrei in an average of about 20 sessions. One female patient was treated 77 times, one male patient 47 times, and two other women received Johrei 45 and 38 times, respectively. Seven patients had less than ten sessions, of whom four were treated only four times.

Such wide variation in frequency of treatment was probably unavoidable, since most of the patients were not permanently hospitalized and visited the institute on an irregular schedule, remaining there only long enough to undergo a series of medical treatments. In some cases they died there. Some of the patients released from the hospital did not return for one reason or another for further treatment. Thus, it was impossible to maintain a regular schedule of Johrei administration. The intervals between sessions often stretched to weeks, even months.

Rev. Tada nonetheless established a warm personal rapport with each of the patients he treated. He found their courage and determination impressive, and in each case they reported an entirely positive, hopeful attitude towards Johrei itself. They looked forward to each session. It was interesting that they became deeply attached to the Japanese pastor, even though his limited conversational English prevented much verbal communication. He was ably assisted by a team of doctors and nurses, some of whom showed a personal interest in treatment by Johrei.

Moral support and cooperation given by the chaplain at the hospital made a significant difference in the willingness shown by the patients to receive Johrei without anxiety. The overall hospital environment, in fact, proved to be unexpectedly free from the scepticism or even animosity towards a "faith healer" that could have arisen, if the management of the project had been less skillful.

Inconclusive Results

The results of the study are contained in "Report of Clinical Experience: Effects of Johrei on Patients with Far Advanced Lung Cancer, 1980–1981," which was compiled in the spring of 1982. In the report the data collected from the interviews are presented and assessed. The average number of interviews for treated patients was 3.4 and for control patients, 3.1. The evaluable data to determine the vitagram score were summarized as initial score, final score, and change in status. Another set of figures was calculated to represent results of the McGill pain questionnaire, and data from the additional quality of life questionnaire were also evaluated.

Evaluable data were less abundant than first anticipated. That obtained in the McGill pain questionnaire, for example, reflected responses from 7 control patients (3 never reported pain, one could complete only the first interview) and 6 treated patients (3 reported pain in only one interview).

A statistical analysis of the limited data indicated an inconclusive result overall; in other words, it could not be concluded that therapy with Johrei was superior or inferior to conventional medical treatment without Johrei. But several factors suggest that the conditions of the experimental treatment were inadequate to produce conclusive results. First of all, the theoretical basis of Johrei, and its preponderant emphasis on spiritual power, would seem to require intensive treatment over a much longer period than was possible in this study, when the disease was so advanced. Not only was the overall experiment period probably too short, but circumstances prevented regular treatment at optimum frequency. Further, it may be that the patients under study did not have a life expectancy long enough to permit observation of the possible beneficial effects of Johrei. Most important, all the patients were receiving significant amounts of analgesics, most commonly opiates and other treatments, which either undermined any effects of Johrei or counteracted them completely. At the very least, analgesics probably masked any alleviation of pain, for example, that Johrei could effect. Thus it can be said that under the prevailing conditions, it was not possible to measure the effects of Johrei alone, or compare the effects of Johrei and conventional treatment. The fact that all the patients had undergone surgery at some time made it difficult to assess the effects of Johrei with any certainty.

Although it was impossible to record clearly positive results at this time, Rev. Tada was satisfied that Johrei had produced no ill effects, physically or subjectively, and the patients treated indicated no emotional or psychological resistance to it. On the contrary, their attitude of hopeful expectancy convinced others outside the group to receive Johrei, and it seemed that in each case, even if there was no marked physical improvement, sessions of Johrei left the patients feeling better and with greater peace of mind. (Apart from the treated patients, a number of other people, whose complaints ranged from chronic headaches to stomach problems, diabetes, and broken bones, received Johrei. Several sessions of Johrei had positive effects in most of these cases.)

Johrei and Mice

During April–June 1981, a related experiment was set up to test a group of 41 mice in which tumors had been transplanted. They were randomized into control and treated groups, and the 20 treated mice were given Johrei regularly. The results yielded no statistically significant differences in length of survival for the two groups, although, as indicated in the final report, the mice in the treated group lived longer than those in the control group during the third phase of the experiment.

In 1982, Rev. Tada decided to conduct in Japan another series of experiments with mice. He believes that transplanted tumors grow too rapidly to allow the beneficial effects of Johrei to work, and he wishes to document the results of Johrei given to mice whose disease progresses more gradually. He is also eager to apply what he learned in the previous experiment, for example, that a mouse requires the administration of Johrei much more frequently than a human being.

Thus, with the assistance of his colleagues and under the supervision of a local cancer specialist, Rev. Tada began a long-term, multilevel study in Kyoto. One level, in which the effect of Johrei on externally-inflicted wounds is measured, has already been administered through two cycles and has yielded two sets of data. The data yielded will be fully analyzed when the entire experiment is completed, but the findings to date are distinctly more favorable to the mice in the treated group than those in the control group.

Another level involves measuring the effect of Johrei on mice that develop spontaneously occurring tumors; none of the tumors will have been transplanted. The progress of the disease in this case is very slow, and no definitive results can be expected for some time. In a third level of the Kyoto study, mice with transplanted tumors will be carefully monitored in an experiment similar to the 1981 test. In addition, plans are being made to test the effects of Johrei on tumors developed from carcinogenic substances, certain types of inflammation, and other induced or spontaneously occurring disorders in mice.

Apart from clinical studies such as the above, there are few, if any, ways to scientifically document the effect of Johrei. People are occasionally tempted to try to measure the electromagnetism emanating from the hand of the administrator, or photograph "waves" generated, but such attempts would probably not be successful, insofar as any "waves" associated with Johrei do not appear to have such properties. It remains true, however, that Johrei has remarkable effects, and those who have experienced them are always ready to testify. The best "proof" lies in the beneficiaries of Johrei, and at this point it is still to them that we must turn to gain the most convincing evidence.

II. Research on Nature Farming

An important part of Mokichi Okada's teachings concerns agriculture. He taught a method of cultivation called nature farming, which is designed to let the soil exercise its inherent power and produce truly natural, pure foodstuffs (see NATURE FARMING, pp. 124–28). Several believers living in farming districts have been trying to follow the teaching, as they understand it, for twenty to thirty years. Kazue Tanaka of Shiga prefecture and Yukiko Isa and Shigesaku Ueda of Kyoto are among those whose persistence and care have been truly remarkable. Although the size of their farms is modest and their understanding of the teaching is still far from perfect, the enormous experimental value of their efforts is becoming more apparent all the time. In fact, about nine years ago, a group of agricultural scientists in the Kyoto-Osaka area began doing research on these nature farming fields and their crops, and their studies are yielding highly important data. Below we will summarize their findings to date, focusing on the paddy field cultivated by Mrs. Tanaka and Mr. Ueda's vegetable fields.

A. Non-manured Rice Fields

Since 1951, Mrs. Tanaka has been practicing nature farming in her 15-are rice field located in Rittō, Shiga prefecture. She has not used synthetic or organic fertilizers, composts, insecticides, or any other kind of agricultural chemicals. Continuous irrigation is the only input she supplies for the paddy. The field produces plants that stand strong against disease and insect damage, and withstand violent weather. The brown rice yield is stable at 40 kg per are, which is about 70% of the yield of the most productive fertilized paddies in the area. The quality of nature-farming rice is superior; when boiled or steamed, it is so delicious that even a sick person who cannot eat anything else finds that it tastes good to him and gives him strength.

Scientists from Kinki University's Faculty of Agriculture,* under the leadership of Professor Hiroshi Hasegawa, have been conducting research on Mrs. Tanaka's field since 1974, using an adjacent manured field as a contrast paddy field. Their main findings to date are as follows:

1 Characteristics of *Beniasahi*

The rice cultivar planted in Mrs. Tanaka's field is *Beniasahi*, a late variety that was developed before World War II and was popular until the early fifties when far less fertilizer was being used than today. Mrs. Tanaka has stayed with *Beniasahi* since she converted to nature farming in 1951. She takes all her seeds from the good hills in her own field. Tests show that in comparison with the high-yield varieties developed more recently, *Beniasahi* is better suited to non-manured farming. It has also been demonstrated that compared with rice from the contrast field, the non-manured paddy field yields rice whose "rice-bran" layer comes off more easily in the polishing process and whose milled grains are firmer and taste better. Moreover, the eating quality of non-manured rice does not deteriorate as much, and is eminently palatable even after two full years.

2 Winter Weeds

A survey done immediately before spring ploughing showed

* Located in Higashi Osaka city, Osaka prefecture.

Mrs. Tanaka's rice field, Ritto, Shiga prefecture

that the non-manured field had produced less than half the winter weeds, weighed after drying, than the contrast field. This means that the non-manured field is deficient in soil nutrients during winter. The manured field, in contrast, produced numerous weeds even when rice straw, chopped by a combine harvester, had been spread over it to restrain the growth of winter weeds there.

3 Rice Plant Growth

Deficiency of nutrients tends to retard growth during the first month after the seedlings are transplanted, which is in early May in the Kyoto-Osaka region. The delay in the development of tillers is especially conspicuous. But as soon as the soil temperature rises in July, the amount of ammonium nitrogen released from the soil increases, giving depth to the color of leaves and accelerating the growth of rice plants.

During the middle and late growth periods, the roots of non-manured rice plants continue to extend, whereas their development stagnates in the contrast field. Consequently, the roots are much larger and longer in nature-farming fields than in fertilized fields. Thus, in terms of growth response, rice plants in the non-manured field demonstrate an "autumn vigor" phenomenon. In the ripening period, all the leaves stand out stiff and straight, which gives the whole plant more exposure to solar radiation and accelerates grain filling.

The relatively lower yield of brown rice in the non-manured field is due to the lag in development of tillers and the consequently smaller number of ears produced. Because the vegetative growth of rice plants is not pushed to excess in the nature-farming field, the amount of solar radiation on the soil surface is much greater than in the contrast field. After late June, the daily maximum soil temperature (5 cm depth) is consistently higher in the non-manured field than in the manured field by 2-4 °C.

4 Planting Density

The leaf area per square meter in the non-manured field is approximately half that in the contrast field. It seemed possible to increase the yield by narrowing the space between the plants. As a result of planting density tests, however, it became clear that the main competing factor in the growth of rice plants in the non-manured field is not sunlight, but the amount of nutrients within the unit area per hill. Thus it is conjectured that even if the number of hills per square meter were increased from the present 19, the yield would probably not rise much, if at all.

5 Nitrogen Supplied from Irrigation Water

The natural sources of nitrogen in paddy fields are primarily irrigation water, soil, and biological nitrogen fixation. In the case of Mrs. Tanaka's rice field, the irrigation water is the most important source. The amount of dissolved ammonium nitrogen in this particular water is 0.224 mg/l, which is a little higher than the average irrigation water in typical agricultural districts. The total nitrogen content in Mrs. Tanaka's irrigation water is 0.941 mg/l, however, indicating that the water contains suspending substances whose nitrogen content is more than three times as high as the dissolved ammonium nitrogen.

One portion of the dissolved ammonium nitrogen is absorbed by the rice plants and microbes, while another portion adsorbs to the soil itself. The suspending substances are spread throughout the field but tend to settle most heavily in areas near the inlet, indicating that the irrigation water carries in a major proportion of the total amount of nitrogen in the soil.

Although the exact ratio has yet to be confirmed, the total volume of water irrigated in Mrs. Tanaka's field is estimated to be 6–10 times greater than in the average rice paddy field. And it is proven that reducing the volume of irrigated water has adverse effects on plant growth and yield, especially in areas close to the inlet.

6 Total Nitrogen in the Soil

A large portion of the total nitrogen content in the soil takes the form of organic nitrogen, and one part of that mineralizes and is absorbed and used by the rice plant. Investigation of non-manured paddy fields shows that the total nitrogen in the soil is always highest at the field inlet, followed by the center, and outlet, in that order. The nitrogen increases gradually after the field has been filled with water, and it reaches almost maximum level by the latter part of July. By harvest time, the total nitrogen in the soil is more or less back to its pre-submersion level. This periodical change in level is caused presumably by the addition of nitrogen carried by the irrigation water and the absorption of nitrogen by the rice plants.

In another survey, the total nitrogen in the central area of manured and non-manured fields in early July was measured and compared for four consecutive years. On the average, the nitrogen in the non-manured field was as high as 70% of that in the manured field. How are we to explain the comparatively high total nitrogen in the non-manured field, and why did the nitrogen content not diminish over a period of four years? The scientists who made the survey conjecture that the greater part of the nitrogen absorbed by the rice plants is constantly replenished by nitrogen contained in the irrigation water.

7 Mineralization of Organic Nitrogen

The degree of mineralization of the organic nitrogen in the soil is measured in terms of the volume of ammonium nitrogen released therefrom. Two types of experiments were conducted in order to estimate the relative amounts of ammonium nitrogen formed in the fertilized and unfertilized fields. First, potential mineralization in soil was tested at 30 °C for ten weeks by the submerged incubation method, and second, the effective heat unit summation of soil temperature (over 15 °C) conducive to mineralization during the growing period of rice plants was obtained. As a result of these tests, where figures for the non-manured soil were consistently higher than those for the manured, the volume of ammonium nitrogen released from the soil is estimated to be about 130% higher in the non-manured field.

8 Biological Nitrogen-fixing Activity

Nitrogen fixation is caused by activity of nitrogen-fixing bacteria in the rhizospheres of rice plants. Nitrogen-fixing activity in manured and non-manured fields was tested repeatedly on the sample roots and soil around rhizospheres by the acetylene reduction method. The same method was also applied to the soil as a whole, and to the roots of rice plants grown in separate pots filled with manured and non-manured soil, respectively. These tests have clearly demonstrated the nitrogen-fixing activity in non-manured fields to be far more vigorous than that in manured fields.

Research has yet to be carried out on the role of blue-green algae found in the field, which are known to photosynthesize. It is conjectured that greater solar radiation on the non-manured soil surface means greater nitrogen-fixing activity by blue-green algae there than in the manured field.

9 Resistance to Blast and Pests

Several blast fungus inoculation tests on samples of the *Beniasahi* variety from non-manured and manured fields have proved that rice plants grown in the former have much greater resistance to blast disease throughout the entire period of growth. It has also been confirmed that an extraordinarily high percent of silicate-accumulated cells in non-manured rice plants during the ripening period functions effectively to check the occurrence of neck blast and others.

Practitioners of nature farming reported that their crops suffered little in 1969 when many manured fields in the area were completely devastated by a massive influx of planthoppers. No scientific investigation was conducted at that time to confirm this. When a similar influx of planthoppers occurred in Kyoto in September 1982, however, agricultural entomologists from Kinki University were able to make a careful comparative study of Mrs. Isa's non-manured paddy fields and the adjacent manured fields in Iwakura. While all the neighboring fields were adversely affected by the influx, no damage was recorded in Mrs. Isa's.

B.   Non-manured Vegetable Fields

No extensive research has been conducted on non-manured vegetable cultivation. Since we do not have abundant scientific data on these, we will present some findings based on observations of Shigesaku Ueda's vegetable fields in Yamashina ward, Kyoto city. In 1971 Mr. Ueda converted part of his paddy area into dry vegetable fields and began growing tomatoes, cucumbers, sweet potatoes, spring onions, Japanese radishes, eggplants, and many others. Following the nature farming method, he used no synthetic fertilizer, agricultural chemicals, or even organic matter such as composts or manure. Moreover, he divided his field into specialized patches so he could repeat the same crop on the same ground.

Unfortunately, the absence of a contrast field in areas close or adjacent to Mr. Ueda's has made it impossible to gather exact comparative data on the mode of plant growth or the quality of produce. Generally, however, we know that the non-manured vegetable farm gives lower yields than the manured, while qualitatively the produce of nature farming is far superior to that of conventional agriculture, which is heavily dependent on fertilizer and chemicals. On the simplest level, it tastes better, is firmer, and satisfies more fully. It seems also to answer certain needs in the human body. We have numerous records of cases when a patient, who is in critical condition and cannot eat anything else, is able to eat and enjoy vegetables grown in non-manured fields.

White radishes and turnips grown by nature farming

invariably develop a higher ratio of root to top, i.e., the leafy portion. The root portion, which we normally consume, of non-manured radishes and turnips is more graceful in shape and the skin is more glossy. Similarly, specialists have testified that sweet potatoes from the non-manured field not only look better but taste better.

Some years ago Mr. Ueda won first prize for his kidney beans in a regional contest. The pods of his kidney beans are shiny and the seeds inside are longer than those from manured produce. His green peas, also, compare favorably with those grown in manured fields in number of peas per pod and weight, although the total yield is smaller.

It took Mr. Ueda four or five years until he finally produced well-rolled cabbages by nature farming. Their leaves are thin and tightly rolled. Hence, the specific gravity of each roll is higher than in the average manured cabbage. Similarly, eggplants grown from non-manured seeds are confirmed to have higher disease resistance than those from manured seeds.

C. The Significance of Nature Farming

As early as the 1930s, Mr. Okada started to encourage nature farming, saying that modern agriculture, because it slights the vital role of natural power inherent in the soil, must be reconsidered in its entirety. In the subsequent fifty years, however, agricultural practices have moved in directions that are diametrically opposed to Mr. Okada's ideas. In the paragraphs below, we call attention to the several ways in which nature farming may contribute to the reorientation of agriculture.

1 Agriculture in Japan has become increasingly dependent on synthetic fertilizer, and concomitantly on agricultural chemicals, both derived primarily from petroleum. The un-

bridled use of petrochemical products plus the widespread mechanization of farm work have increased the necessary input of energy enormously. In fact, in relative terms, the input exceeds the output in value. Mineral reserves are finite, but man must continue to produce food as long as he survives. Agriculture that consumes so much energy clearly undermines efforts towards a common goal of our time—energy conservation.

Just the fact that Mrs. Tanaka's non-manured field has a far richer natural supply of nitrogen than the contrast field suggests that nature farming is a feasible, practical alternative to today's energy-consuming methods of cultivation.

2 Excessive use of chemicals in agriculture has also led to serious environmental disruption by polluting soil and water. There is no way to stop the destruction and restore health to our environment unless, at the very least, we cut down on our use of chemical fertilizers, pesticides, herbicides, and other agricultural chemicals. Actually, with some extra effort for weeding, we can eliminate the use of chemicals altogether, as the non-manured paddy fields of Mrs. Tanaka and others demonstrate. Those fields have not only produced a stable, albeit modest, yield over the years and a crop that is resistant to blast and harmful insects, but they have provided food that is pure, strengthening, and delicious. It should also be possible to drastically reduce the intensive labor required for weeding in the not-too-distant future when an appropriate machine or some other nonchemical method is devised.

3 In recent years consumers have complained about the damage to health caused by residual poisons from agricultural chemicals. As this became a widespread issue, more and more people began to favor natural foods, or health foods, free from

artificial preservatives, additives, or any other kind of chemical. Nature farming offers us hope for a solution here, too, for its products are pure and of superior quality, and they keep for a longer time without preservatives. Even seriously ill people find them palatable. At present, nature farming fields yield a little less in quantity than manured fields, but in quality their produce is purer even than most "natural foods" or "health foods" because no compost or fertilizer of any kind has been used.

4   Scientific research has confirmed that the presence of chemical inorganic nitrogen tends to inhibit biological nitrogen fixation. Research by Dr. Hasegawa and his colleagues on non-manured paddy fields has verified this. Mr. Okada's admonition against the use of any fertilizers or chemicals, in order to fully activate and exploit the natural power of soil, has been partly proved to be scientifically valid. But further research and help from agricultural scientists are now necessary to improve the cultivation techniques and raise the productivity of nature farming.

5   Medical scientists and nutritionists, for their part, can make a major contribution by studying and comparing the effects of foodstuffs produced without fertilizer or chemicals on the health of consumers. Specifically, scientific investigation is needed to determine exactly why a seriously ill patient finds the produce of nature farming so palatable, even when he or she is too weak to eat anything else.

6   The roots and leaves of rice plants grown in Mrs. Tanaka's non-manured field are healthier and stronger than those of the contrast field. The non-manured plants are also more resistant to disease, as we have seen. The more natural the nutrition of the plant, the healthier it apparently is.

To what extent does this principle apply to the human body? What are the effects on human health, both short and long term, of food additives, chemicals, medicines, and other foreign substances taken into the body? These questions merit much more serious research by medical scientists and pharmacologists.

Mr. Okada's teaching on nature farming, as well as on human health in general, suggests new directions for and opens up new horizons in scientific research in a number of fields, especially those directly concerned with life. If the necessary research is carried out, it will make a great contritution to the well-being of mankind.

Index

of 14, 39, 64, 69: will of 40–41, 45ff., 52, 62–63, 70, 75ff., 84, 191, 200, 202ff., 209, 212; works of 57, 192, 196, 203
godliness 49, 57, 82
good 36–38, 47, 49, 52, 57ff., 79–80, 198–99, 201
good works 69
grace 38, 67, 74, 78–79, 191, 194, 209; fall from 35, 52, 199
Greater Japan Society of Kannon 164–66
greed 77, 207
growth 44
guardian spirit 49–50

Hakone Museum 168
happiness 35, 38, 75–76, 87, 212
harmony 73–74, 81, 191
hatred 53, 201
healing 20–22, 95, 111, 116, 144, 192–93
health 22ff. 70, 81, 88, 91ff., 99–101, 108ff., 120–21, 123–24, 127–28, 232–34
heart (physical) 98, 100; (spiritual) 45ff., 53, 75, 83, 206–7
heaven 44, 82, 87, 191
henotheism 12fn.
herbs 93, 107, 122
Hippocrates 92, 94
history 17, 32, 36–37, 65, 70–71, 204; Japanese 13, 16
homicide 207
hope 35, 99, 195, 203
horizontal principle 72
human body 23, 43–44, 88–89, 127
human race 32, 51, 58, 89

human relations 74
humanity 55, 71, 80
humankind (mankind) 18, 22, 26, 33–34, 41, 58, 66, 68, 107, 179, 188, 234
humility 78, 198

impurities 23, 25, 43, 52, 62, 89, 91–92, 95–96, 99, 114–15, 120, 126
individual 210
individualism 72
infection 103, 107
injustice 37, 207
inspirations 17, 19, 79, 196
intellect 47, 89, 206–7
intelligence 198
interest, conflict of 74

Japan 17–18, 179, 204
Japan Kannon Church 170, 175
Japanese, people 12ff., 164; society 14, 16–17, 175
jealousy 49, 201, 207
Jesus 9, 58–59
Johrei 9–10, 35, 60, 73, 77, 99, 111, 133, 165–67, 171, 180–82, 197, 209, 215ff.; effectiveness of 43, 64, 69, 110; as a gift 12, 22, 54–55, 66, 70, 91, 115, 190, 193; as a healing method 14–15, 20–21, 82–83, 89, 103, 105, 116ff.; and repentance 67–68, 201, 203; as a sign 70–71, 79, 195, 205
judgment 18–19, 34, 54, 65, 75, 80, 82, 140, 195, 203–4
justice 74